Dedicated to
my wonderful
sister **Rives**

Hamburger²

Sunny Side of South Elm and Poole's Paradise
first appeared in O.Henry magazine.

Written, designed, produced by Billy Ingram

Contact: Billy@TVparty.com

ISBN-13: 978-1502996572
ISBN-10: 150299657X
BISAC: History / United States / State & Local / South

The Sunny Side of the Street

During Downtown Greensboro's heyday, the 1940s and '50s, Packards and DeSotos jammed the streets jockeying for parking spaces, massive neon signs obliterated the night sky, dazzling shoppers with movement and color. Towering hotels, multi-layered department stores, elegant fashion boutiques, men's furnishings, car dealerships, four movie theaters, some 700 businesses generating hundreds of millions of dollars from early morning until 9:00pm when they rolled up the sidewalks.

In the early 1970s it all unravelled with alarming speed. In an attempt to create a mall-like experience the city covered over a majority of the parking spaces on Elm Street to widened the sidewalks. Within a couple of years downtown was two tumbleweeds short of a ghost town. Despite the recent boom in nightclubs and eateries a major portion of South Elm Street has remained in a state of neglect with magnificent architectural treasures languishing—but doing so in their original states. Monuments to the gods of retail on the western side of the 300 block of South Elm erected between 1886 and 1927 are just now being resurrected.

Constructed just prior to the turn of the last century 304 South Elm was named for contractor W.C. Bain, responsible for many of Greensboro's more elaborate center city retail hubs. The top two floors, accentuated by large arched windows and sculpted terra cotta overlays, was where dentist Dr. Walter Hartsell and barber George Sleight drilled and chilled throughout the 1930s & '40s. In the 1950s J Lee Stone photographed bridal and baby portraits in his spacious studio.

The inviting storefront below features 3 dramatic glass showcases and transoms, all framed with impressive cast iron columns. By far the Bain Building's most soulful resident was the Greensboro Record Center, from the go-go sixties into the eighties a musical epicenter with one of the largest selections of oldies 45s imaginable. City councilwoman Nancy Hoffman rescued this derelict in 2013, undertaking a complete overhaul, restoring the handsome Neo-Classical metalwork and simple wooden door frames. It is once again an entertainment destination, Scuppernong's, a relaxing wine bar/bookstore. Owner Brian Lampkin explained why here and now, "Largely it was what was missing in our own lives. What do we want or expect from a city that wasn't here? Bookstores have been a center of information, of friendship, of great personal value. We knew we weren't alone. There's a guy who was 11 years old sweeping floors here in the 1930s, now he comes in, he's in his late eighties, and reminisces with us. I guess it was his grandfather's store."

The Grissom Building next door at 310 has also been reanimated with luxury accommodations upstairs. Designed by J. H. Hopkins it's a spectacular three-story example of the Italianate style predominant on this block, highlighted by cascading Romanesque brickwork surrounding palatial window arches augmented with stone half-columns and sills.

Like its neighbor, the ground level is framed in decorative cast iron. Built in 1899 for Grissom's Drug Store this was Cecil-Russell Drugs in the 1930s and '40s, a Goodwill store and Coats Ltd. in the 1970s.

Rich in Beau-Arts inspired details, with windows crowned by stained glass semi-circles and fanciful concrete sills, 312 South Elm will be restored to her former glory over the next few months thanks to developers Dawn Chaney and Pam Frye. Dawn shared their plans, "The building was Burtner's Furniture, they were in there until about 1980, that's when The Book Trader moved in. We're going to put retail on the first floor, that's about 3,500 square feet, and then on the second and third floors will be loft apartments and we're going to call them Book Trader Lofts. We will have two 2 bedroom, 2 bath, and four 1 bedroom, all with windows to the exterior." Chaney owns dozens of historically significant commercial and residential units, she bought her first property downtown in 1979, "I can't tell you how many people came to me and said, "You're making a mistake Dawn, something's going to happen to you over there, that area is not safe. It was the low life that lived here. People renting rooms, do I need to say much more? Hell's Angels lived here and had motorcycles up in the middle of the front room. But look what a dream can do. I want to help make Greensboro the number one city in the state of North Carolina, it will take a team."

A galvanized cornice crowns 314-316, the largest and most formidable on the block, four stories fronted by rugged carved granite stones above two enormous retail spaces. It was built in 1904 for M. G. Newell, seller of buggies and bicycles, an early distributor for a new motorized bike called Harley-Davidson. S. H. Kress was located in 316 before expanding a block north in 1929. The top 3 floors have new windows installed but the interior hasn't yet been refurbished. The storefronts, both presently empty, were last remodeled in the 1930's when Miller Furniture opened their doors. Last of the 'Furniture Row' dinosaurs, Miller's only recently closed.

One of Greensboro's first department stores, The New York Racket, opened in 1892 at 318 South Elm. Clothing merchant A.V. Sapp ("Sells It Cheap") did business here for 25 years beginning in 1905; over a century later his bold painted mural on the front of the building still screams out across the boulevard. Boomers will fondly recall Tiny Town Toyland, owned and operated by a charming Cuban couple Harry & Faye Rimsky. Merchandise they didn't sell stayed on the shelves so metal cars and talking dolls dating back to the fifties were displayed alongside the latest offerings. After a run of 20 years this mom and pop shop closed in the mid-1970s.

It may be christened The Fortune Building but 320 was a revolving door for furnishings and fashion, the longest tenant she's ever had is the one that's there now. When everyone else was hightailing it, Bill Heroy bought this dusty jewel in 1977 for $30,000 then lovingly refurbished it for his Old Photo Specialist studio. "I've always loved downtown, my wife and I used to walk our kids around here when they were two and three. It was like being in the country, on a Sunday I'd look out my window and never see a car. I spent almost $2,000,000 rehabbing this building. We actually blew our roof out to put bedrooms on top of the building. We opened that in 1988 and I'll bet we've had less that a half of a percent vacancy since then."

342-344, currently hosting Design Archives, was constructed in 1890 then modernized in 1924 for the Gate City Hotel, that's when Fleisher Brothers Clothing and Coble Hardware (later Sporting Goods) moved into the retail units underneath. Congressman Howard Coble recalls, "Jack Coble, who was no relation but a very good friend, he used to come and watch our baseball games at Alamance High School. He had a horse and a carriage, a little buggy, he would ride right out into our ball field during the game. Very colorful guy Jack Coble was." You can still read the name of the store in the tile welcome mat outside the front door. Modern offices are above.

For generations the intersection of South Elm and McGee has been known as 'Hamburger Square' where Jim's Lunch, California Sandwich Shop, Princess Cafe, and the New York Cafe were located for decades. The upper floors and rear of 346 have been repurposed as bars—O'Coul's, Green Burro, and Longshanks—but the corner spot where Jim's Lunch held forth for 40+ years has never experienced a major renovation after serving their last in 1976. Within a year even the trains wouldn't stop downtown any longer.

The trains are back, so are the crowds. The rich history and traditions of South Elm are on track to be preserved for future generations to be inspired by. And yes, you can get a hamburger again in Hamburger Square, darn good ones, at the Snack Bar in the former site of the New York Cafe, or at Natty Greene's where the California Sandwich Shop first buttered their buns back in 1934.

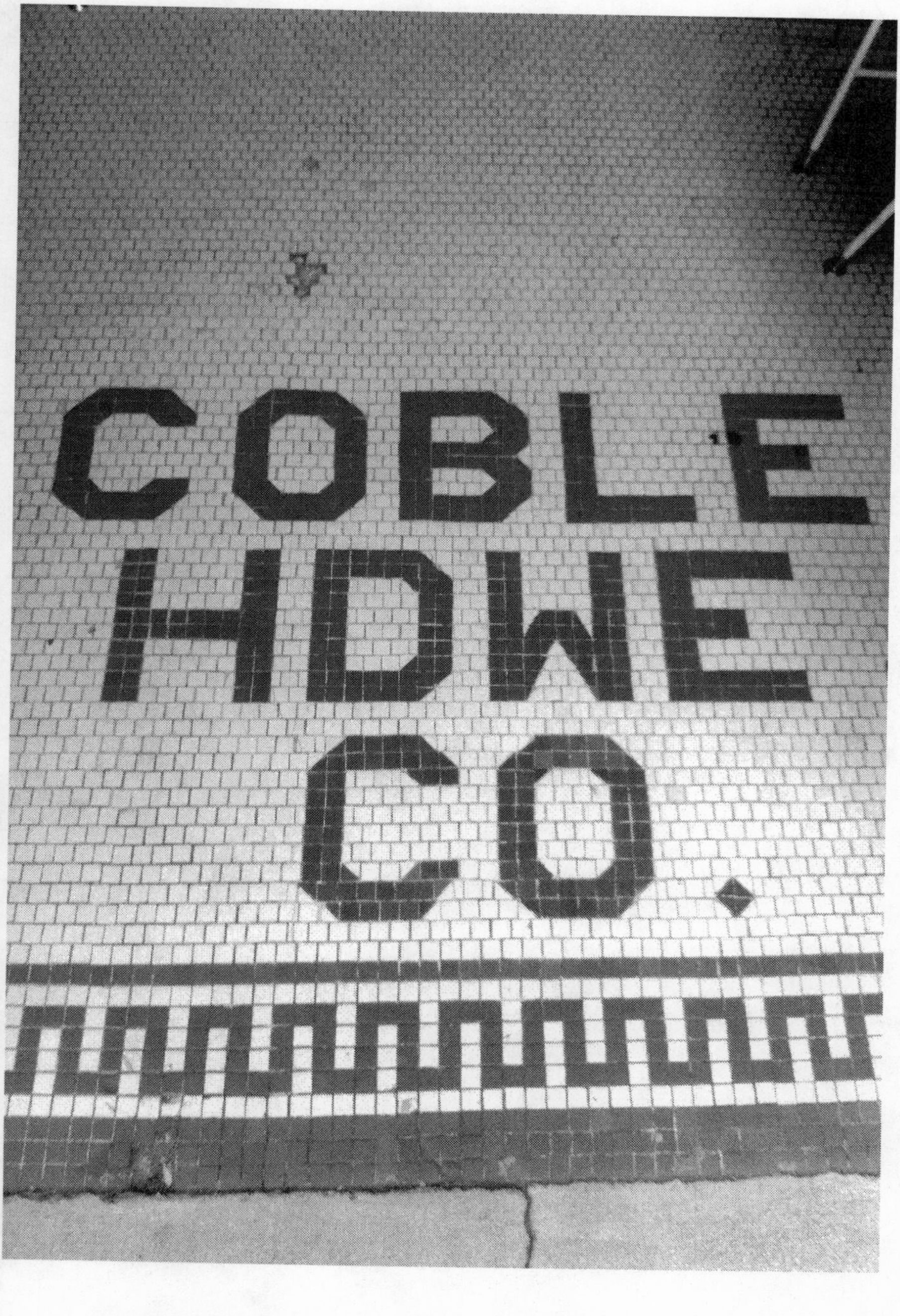
COBLE
HDWE.
CO.

Poole's Paradise

In 1946 Jesse Robert Poole, a Stoneville native with a midnight to 1 a.m. shift on a clear channel signal echoing off Lake Pontchartrain, unwittingly ignited a revolution when he seized upon a federal court order allowing phonograph records to be played over the airwaves. Radio up to that time had been all about live music, with local stations employing their own orchestras and bands. Broadcasting from New Orleans Bob Poole's on-air combo, The Salty Five, included Pete Fountain, Al Hirt and other Preservation Hall jazzbos.

By blending recordings from across the musical spectrum with crazy sound effects like a street car roaring through the studio, a woman's scream or repetitious hyena shrieks after a corny joke — and all of Bob's jokes were straight off the husk — the modern disc jockey emerged from the primordial static.

Bob Poole & Willie

One mid-1940s listener gushed, "Through Poole's anarchistic humor and juxtapositions of sound and anarchy he created an existential bond between me and the world." L. W. Milam of Ralph magazine was another early fan, "American radio was far more inspired in those days. Television had come along and everyone was concentrating on it. Network radio was dwindling; local live radio was blossoming. For a few years that meant a freedom on AM radio that allowed people to be loose, chatty and friendly; to be themselves. This was brought to high art by Bob Poole at WWL, Jean Shepherd in New York City and the young Arthur Godfrey in Washington, D.C."

Bob met his wife Gloria a few years earlier. While serving in the Navy,

he crashed a posh soirée the urban sophisticate was hosting for the New Orleans Symphony. They were married three months later. She recalls the ebullient post-war era when "Poole's Paradise" became for 1940s audiences what "Saturday Night Live" was to the 1970s: "Bob was heard all over the United States and Canada. He had a studio audience so many people wanted to see him." WWL was located in the elegant Roosevelt Hotel, Frank Sinatra and all the biggest stars performed in the showroom there. Gloria would ride the elevator to the top floor and wait for Bob's show to be over, "then we would go to a place across the street called the 1-2-3 Bar. Dick Clark was just a little sassy kid then but he took a liking to Bob, so he'd come too and pester us to death. Bob would have to tell him, 'Go home, Dick.' But he was a nice little fellow."

Of her first visit to Greensboro, Gloria says, "We came on the train; this was right after the war. We stayed at the O.Henry Hotel. There was a railroad car out in front that served as a diner. I thought this was a funny little town. They didn't sell whiskey, which of course, Bob loved greatly, but the O.Henry had a bellboy named 'Snag.' So first thing he'd send that guy out to find wherever they were selling it."

Bob Poole, and a small handful of others, not only ushered in a new era of radio entertainment, they sparked a genuine craze among the nation's hep cats and bobbysoxers — deejays were no longer staid announcers but the nation's hit makers and trend setters. The Mutual network took notice, luring "Poole's Paradise" from The Big Easy to The Big Apple in 1948 for an hour weekday afternoons at 3. The show was an immediate smash, so much so Mutual awarded Bob with a morning timeslot and a half-hour in primetime. He was voted Disc Jockey's Favorite Disc Jockey in 1949 and 1950, garnering more than four times as many votes as future "Tonight" show host Steve Allen. For three years running, he captured Billboard magazine's top DJ award.

After four successful seasons on Mutual, Bob Poole found himself at the crossroads — move into television like his contemporaries or embrace the inevitability that all radio would eventually be local. 'The Duke of Stoneville' made the decision to return to his roots, Major Edney Ridge's 1470 AM WBIG. He'd gotten his start there while attending Guilford College back in 1934, hosting a country music show with the Southern Pioneers and providing color commentary for the very first Greater Greensboro Open in 1938.

"She said she felt like a young colt but she looked more like an old 45." — Bob Poole

"Poole's Paradise" debuted on WBIG (We Believe in Greensboro) in the fall of 1952, broadcast from a studio a floor below the lobby in the magnificently appointed O.Henry Hotel on the corner of Elm and Bellemeade. Bob, with his engineer and comic foil Willie (Dailey) served up a blend of news, weather, sports, novelty tunes like Ginny Simm's "If I Knew You Were Coming I'd've Baked a Cake," all peppered with a heapin' helpin' of Bob's bad puns. It was small town hokum simmered with big city heat and the public ate it up. 70 percent of Greensboro's morning radio audience tuned to "Poole's Paradise" from 6–9:30 a.m.

Gloria remembers, "Major Edney Ridge was a colorful character. He had a girlfriend — though he was married — and her name was Maggie. He and

Bob would have knock-down, drag-out arguments where the Major would say, 'You're fired, get out,' and Bob would say, 'Fine' and walk out and the next day they'd start all over again. One time the Major said to him, 'You're fired, get out, take what you want with you.' And Bob told him, 'I'll take Maggie!'"

Bill Maudlin (not the cartoonist) was an intern for WBIG at the O.Henry in the '50s, "When you came through the big front doors, you took the steps down one level. Management offices were on the right as you entered, studios were next, behind that was the control room where Willie worked the board. Next in line was the large room where Bob would be. When I was there Dick McAdoo was on afternoons, Bill Neal was the staff announcer; Add Penfield did the evening news and sports at 6 p.m."

An inveterate partier Bob outfitted his own nightclub on wheels, one he shared with my parents and Alan Wannamaker, WBIG's station manager. Gloria recalls, "Bill [Ingram of Ingram Motors] got us an old school bus. We painted it turquoise and orange and I decorated it. We had all the seats taken out and banquet chairs and a bar put in. We'd go to football games or drive around to people's houses, park in their driveway and throw a little cocktail party. At that time you could do all sorts of things you wouldn't dare do today."

When I was a toddler my father brought me along to the WBIG studios, as Bob launched into his theme song I began whistling along with him, causing him to burst out laughing. Not uncommon today but back when broadcasters took great pride in never losing control while on the air, he never let me forget that.

"She was only an optician's daughter — but two glasses and she made a spectacle of herself."

In 1957 WBIG moved to an Edward Loewenstein-designed modernist one story brick and glass structure erected on the outskirts of town. A miniature pool table was mounted on the outer door to the "Poole Roome," Bob's private studio. The program was so hot he could pick and choose advertisers. Even though the station's meager 5,000 watt signal wasn't heard much outside city limits, a 1962 Twist contest he hosted attracted nearly 3,000 participants. Thousands more turned out for "Bob Poole Day" that same year.

Greensboro radio personality Dusty Dunn was whirling stacks of wax in the afternoons at upstart WCOG in 1966. "For Greensboro and Guilford County, WBIG was everyone's main source of information. The whole thing was Bob Poole," Dunn recalls. "He was just as important in Greensboro as the mayor or anybody else. I mean he was the man." Dunn remembers running into Poole at the Carolina Theatre emceeing some sort of promotional event for kids. "He was really phenomenal. He really had a sharp wit about him. I realized then that [the reason] he was so good on the radio and popular for so many years was because he was so funny."

Changing musical styles and FM radio began encroaching on AM's dominance in the early-1970s but the popularity of "Poole's Paradise" continued unabated. In 1970 a 45-rpm single was released of Bob cheerfully whistling his theme song with "White Azaleas" on the flip side. Asked about it Gloria laughs, "Would you believe I still get asked where to find a copy of "White Azaleas?" After all these years."

"Nobody else had the power he had." Dusty Dunn says, "The guy who managed Sears when it was on Lawndale told me Bob Poole was there doing a remote and mentioned they had copies of 'White Azaleas' they were going to give away, first-come first-served. That store just erupted, everybody was running for the record display. People were knocking over stuff. It was just pandemonium. It was as if Elvis had walked into the building."

WBIG had an exclusive lock on the GGO tournament, now known as the Wyndham Championship, until the late 1960s when the CBS network signed on with avid golfer Bob Poole providing the play-by-play. Andy Durham of GreensboroSports.com was a listener in the 1970s: "They were the flagship station for Carolina Cougars games with the 'Mouth of the South' Bill Curry and Bob Lamey, who now does the Indiana Pacers games on 1070 [AM] out of Indianapolis. WBIG had the first sports call-in show in the area. It started as a Carolina Cougars show with Bones McKinney. After the Cougars fired Bones as coach, he stayed around to do 'Let's Talk Sports' Monday nights at 7 p.m. They carried high school football and other games over the years with announcers like Henry Boggan, Jim Pritchett, Larry Dunlap and Bob Licht."

"He said slip on anything and come on down. So she slipped on the top stair."

In fall of 1973 Bob Poole suffered a series of heart attacks at age 57, hovering between life and death for eight months with family at his bedside. When he returned to the microphone in the summer of '74 it was kept secret that, far too often, "Poole's Paradise" emanated from a room at Cone Hospital.

While in high school I occasionally provided Bob with trivia books and jokes to use on his show, which he greatly appreciated. When "The Manhattan Transfer" LP was released in 1975 I brought him a copy, thinking their jazzy vocalese would be a great fit for his program. He loved the album but confessed he could no longer play the tunes he wanted. Management controlled the music. It obviously stung but I had no way of knowing how much a blow that must have been to the guy who could make or break a record on a national scale earlier in his career. When Manhattan Transfer scored a Top 40 hit a few weeks later he called me on the phone crowing, "They're gonna let me play that record you gave me now!"

The creative visionary who's smoky baritone voice brightened Greensboro's early hours for a quarter century passed away at age 61 on January 24, 1978, a month after his last broadcast. It's not an exaggeration to say the city was in shock. It was front page news, the service carried live from First Presbyterian Church. Inscribed on his stone in Forest Lawn Cemetery are the words Bob Poole left listeners with each morning. "Take care of you, for me."

Another Dip into the Poole

After two years at Guilford College Bob transferred to UNC in Chapel Hill, hitchhiking back to the Gate City for his radio shifts. After dropping out he went on full time at WBIG before landing his first network program. This was before the war. As Bob told it, "After I had been working for WBIG about a year I got to wondering what the the world was like outside of North Carolina. So I went to New York. My boss knew some fellows in the broadcasting business up there.

"I only wanted to visit... but both CBS and NBC shoved me into a studio with a stack of records in front of me and told me to do my stuff. There was nothing to do but take the audition as a good natured joke and go through with it. So for an hour and a half I made up spontaneous wisecracks, referring to programs on other stations and to the station manager as a flop-eared animal."

CBS liked what they heard, summoning Bob back to New York City to star in 'A Southern Boy and a Southern Girl,' a light comedy costarring a budding new musical talent, Dinah Shore. After 13 weeks they were dropped for being, "too Southern."

Then Uncle Sam beckoned. Stationed at the Naval Air Station in New Orleans during WWII Bob's baritone vocals gave weight to 'Sky Wave to Victory' and other patriotic broadcasts heard over 50,000 watt WWL, a free channel station with a nationwide reach. After his stint in the Navy Bob remained at WWL to launch the show in 1945 he would do for the rest of his life, 'Poole's Paradise.'

While Bob broadcast his Mutual program from the Big Apple starting in 1948 he was not heard in New York. By the time he left in 1952 the Mutual network was beginning to unravel. Imitators were flooding the airwaves all around the USA in favor of expensive network programs. That's when Bob Poole made the decision to return to his radio roots, WBIG.

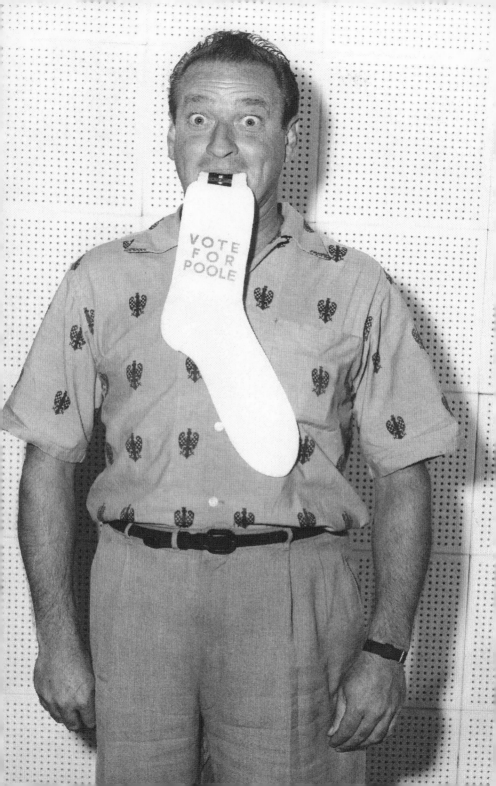

One More Lap Around the Poole

Bob Poole was teamed with kiddie star George Perry for a live broadcast over WBIG on Saturday mornings from the Carolina Circle Mall in the summer of 1977. Bob was having serious health problems and The Old Rebel's TV show had just been cancelled. George Perry was doing occasional segments on the Channel 2 news (Charles Kuralt style) but neither of them looked terribly comfortable in this format. Bob Poole was a radio guy in ill-health suddenly working with an audience, The Old Rebel was a children's host with an audience full of old people.

Dusty Dunn recalls, "It was like something you would do on TV, they had a girl out there who held up cards telling people when to clap, it was a well produced show. It was a theatrical kind of a deal, they talked about what was going on, told jokes and gave away sausage and gravy biscuits.

"I had been working afternoons at WCOG and I went to WRQK, the morning guy left and they gave me the morning show. Bob found out about it somehow, he said to me in that gravelly voice, 'Dusty, this morning thing—the whole secret is, you gotta take a bath every day.' He was just as friendly as he could be."

After Bob passed away Dusty Dunn stepped into the role of Greensboro's AM go-to guy. "When I was negotiating my contract at BIG the girl was going over what I was to get, what I needed, and she asked, 'Do you want batteries? Would that be included in your package?' I said, 'Batteries? Batteries for what?' She said, 'Well, we gave Bob Poole batteries for his flashlight when he wakes up in the morning so he didn't have to turn on the lights and wake his wife up.' I couldn't believe it."

Where Business is Good

Turn west on Edney Ridge Road near the intersection of Battleground and Pisgah Church; at the crest of the hill, look to your right. That's where WBIG sat atop acres of sprawling green lawn peppered with dogwoods, apple trees, and neatly trimmed azaleas—what is now Lowe's Home Improvement and the houses behind.

The property WBIG occupied above a rapidly expanding Battleground Avenue became infinitely more valuable to Jefferson Pilot than a radio signal that couldn't reach much past the city limits. On November 20, 1986, three months after the station's 60th anniversary, with only a few hours notice, a distraught Dusty Dunn fielded calls over the air from disbelieving listeners before the station's signal reverted to static at 6:00pm.

Neighborhood Barnstormer Turned WWII Ace

A hero straight out of central casting, handsome with a Clark Gable smile, World War II fighter pilot George Preddy scored 26.83 air-to-air kills, America's greatest Mustang ace. With "Cripes A' Mighty!" emblazoned on the side of his P-51 Mustang he led The Blue-Nosed Bastards of Bodney to establish total domination over German skies. On a single sortie in August, 1944 he blew 6 Luftwaffe fighters out of the sky, after which he vowed never again to take flight with a hangover.

That Christmas morning the fearless 25-year old dogfighter had just obliterated two Me-109s when he engaged a lone FW-190 strafing Allied forces. Undetected, he attacked the bandit at treetop height just as American ack-ack opened fire. A .50-caliber shell tore through Preddy's aircraft, he was killed in the resulting crash.

Greeksboro

In 1934 Nicholas Kontoulas and his two brothers established California Sandwich Shop on the northeastern corner of South Elm and Edward's Place (now McGee), where Natty Greene's is today. At the same time James Kappas opened Jim's Lunch directly across the street. Soon a rivalry broke out between the two joints over who sold the tastiest hot dogs. So it's kind of ironic they were the inspiration for this intersection's nickname: 'Hamburger Square.'

Fifteen years later, bewildered and alone, teenager Minas Dascalakis landed on these shores from central Greece, a nation ravaged by back-to-back wars with both the Italians and Germans, followed closely by a brutal civil war. Dascalakis spoke to the News & Record about arriving in Greensboro in 1949, "I got a job washing dishes in my brother-in-law's cafe. I worked 5 years for him. He ran a restaurant on South Elm Street, the Princess Cafe. Why a restaurant? That's the only thing I knew then. Where else can a Greek get a job? Where you have a helping hand. When the first immigrants came over, they got into the business and it kept perpetuating."

Boy, did it—by the 1950s there were some 76 eateries in downtown Greensboro alone, almost every one owned by members of the local Greek community, staffed by a phalanx of waiters and cooks mainly from the Evrytania region of Greece.

Greensboro was bursting at the seams in the nifty fifties, a ripple effect from hosting the Overseas Replacement Depot (ORD), an enormous Army Air Force base that processed tens of thousands of troops to fight the Nazis in Europe, then reintegrated them into civilian life once the war was won. A good number of soldiers had no reason to leave the area; as a result, downtown was home to more than a dozen hotels and rooming houses, both large and small.

Thousands of businessmen in loose suits and fedoras shared the sidewalks with scores of ladies in pleated skirts descending on the many jewelry, clothing, and department stores; an attractive setting for coffee shops and luncheonettes.

After years scrimping and saving Minas Dascalakis purchased a short order diner at 223 North Elm from Matthew Pappas in 1953. The very next day it was Minas' behind the counter taking orders at Matthew's Grill ("The Right Place to Eat"); he and his wife Sortiria plated sausage, eggs, and steaks there for the next 34 years.

The Sunday Special at Matthew's was braised rabbit with 2 vegetables, a homemade dessert, and coffee for $1.50. Every day country style steak was served with a couple of sides, a slice of pie and a cup of java for 95 cents. The produce couldn't have been fresher, local farmers pulled their pickup trucks right up to the back door in the mornings so Minas could select the very best for that day's offerings. Business was good, before long he bought the fabled California Sandwich Shop; the original owner and his son James Kontoulos stayed on to run things.

I recently spoke with veteran restauranteur Minas Dascalakis about Greensboro's gilded age, and why Hamburger Square was such a prime location for food service. "The 300 block of South Elm was one of the most lively of the city. In that area there were several small hotels, no more than ten rooms, twelve rooms." Within a two block radius there was the MacArthur Hotel, the Carolina, and the Princess Hotel above California Sandwich. There were rooms for rent above Sam & Mack's Newsstand and other nearby storefronts.

Up the block from California Sandwich, "The Princess Cafe in those days was the elite place to eat. The food was good, the location was right." The cuisine where Minas got his start washing dishes years earlier was traditional, with thick gravy and sauces, known then as Plantation Style. Both Matthew's and the Princess butchered their own meats on the premises, pork fat sizzled in the fryers.

The streets may have been frenzied with shoppers but when people stopped by places like Matthew's Grill it was a relaxed atmosphere, patrons were free to use the restaurants' rear doors rather than hoofing it around to the front.

KING COTTON HOTEL, 250 ROOMS AND BATHS, GREENSBORO, N. C.

Minas benefitted from being just two short blocks from Greensboro's premier hotel, the King Cotton. That venture had an inauspicious debut in 1926, "Where the Guilford Building is now (301 South Elm), the backside was stables for the horses and buggies, that's where everybody parked. They decided to build a hotel there because the O.Henry Hotel was getting a little age. So they built the building you see now for a hotel, a beautiful hotel from what they say... it didn't last but two weeks."

On a hill towering above the train depot vibrations, combined with the cacophony brought on by wheels on steel grinding to a halt, made sleeping impossible. "Those days the railroad was so active, maybe they have almost one hundred trains every day. They loaded the cotton in New Orleans, by the time they reached Greensboro, it's sometimes 2:00 or 3:00 in the morning. That's why they went bankrupt [in two weeks]. Then they went two blocks down and built the King Cotton hotel on Davie."

No Bunkie, Ikea wasn't the first to mix food and retail. 5 and 10 cent stores all had busy lunch counters in the 1950s, drug emporiums did as well. At Woolworths the most expensive item on the menu was a toasted, triple-decker Chicken Salad Sandwich for 65 cents; a De Luxe Tulip Sundae would set you back a quarter.

You could browse the aisles at Belks in Jefferson Square (the corner of Elm and Market) then slide into a booth in the S&W Cafeteria located in the back. Well, you could if you were white. Jefferson Square was the site of mass protests in 1963, when some cafeterias stubbornly refused to integrate after Kress, Woolworths, and other department stores gave in to reason a few years earlier. The S&W closed soon after.

There were also less conventional vendors to contend with operating across from the King Cotton, in storefronts only ten or twelve feet wide.

"You had all those tiny door-to-door situations." Dascalakis recalls, "There was a restaurant in every door. One would have a stool, one would have no stool, the other one have three stools. One guy had chitlins, one guy pig's feet. They specialized, that's how they made a living. They go home and cook twenty pig's feet, they come in to sell them, they go back home and cook again, then come back. There was nobody, [no health department].

"On the other side, before you get down to Davie Street, there were a little bit bigger stores. You could sit down and have some barbeque, another had beef stew, or hot dogs, or chicken, whatever they could put together."

"You go down East Market Street there is a bridge, you know what they used to call it? The Bullpen. You're supposed to be like a bull to go through, that's how rough it was. Always had two police officers. One very big guy was Lt. Mitchum, he could pick up a 200 pound man, lift him up, and throw him on the ground. There were no questions, no questions. There was another officer, a black man about 350 in weight, on the other side of the Bullpen."

Other than the pool halls on South Elm there wasn't much in the way of nightlife—unless you count Mary's Hotel and Restaurant where they didn't just take your reservations, they took your bets in the basement while call girls roamed the halls upstairs.

Alas, every boom has its bust. The Gate City's contraction kicked into high gear in 1973 after the controlled demolition of the King Cotton who's thirteen floors were, in an instant, reduced to a pile of rubble to make way for the News & Record's current digs. Mary's was flattened for a parking lot.

Over at Elm and Bellemeade the O.Henry Hotel's three hundred rooms and stunning art deco lobby had fallen into disrepair and ill repute. At one time the cosmopolitan symbol of a small Southern town's determination to be taken seriously, this crumbling structure's few tenants in the seventies consisted mostly of vagrants and soon to be divorcees, a beacon of squalor in the heart of town. The plan to put the O.Henry out of its misery was first hatched around the block... at Matthew's Grill.

Minas Dascalakis explains, "A friend of mine was assistant manager to the city, he comes into the restaurant one night and he says, 'We got $300,000, community development money, and we don't know what to do with it.' I was talking to the officials just like I was with them. I said, 'Mike, why don't we do something here with that rathole [the O.Henry] up here?' He went back to Mr. Metzger, the director of public works, he talked to him and he called General Townsend, he was the past city manager, they named the

lake in his honor. He talked to him. The next morning he come in, I didn't even unlock the door yet, 'You know, you might have something there.'

"Okay. The city bought the hotel, city destroyed the hotel. Southern Life Insurance Company came in with the cooperation of the city, you know how that works, politics, they bought the property where the hotel was.

"I was on a committee at that time, we wanted to put three floors below Elm Street for a parking deck, one floor on Elm Street for retail, a mall type of space. [The new city manager] was very much against it. He didn't last, I tell you that. He took his shoes and left. If he allowed that almost 200,000 square feet to become retail on that corner, and have two floors on top of them for offices, and three decks below for parking, downtown Greensboro would look different from today."

To hear Minas Dascalakis describe life in Greece during the wars go to: YouTube.com/tvp33

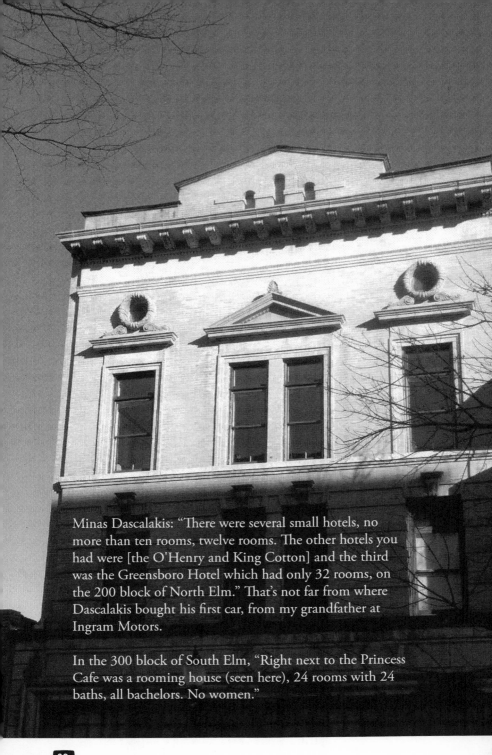

Minas Dascalakis: "There were several small hotels, no more than ten rooms, twelve rooms. The other hotels you had were [the O'Henry and King Cotton] and the third was the Greensboro Hotel which had only 32 rooms, on the 200 block of North Elm." That's not far from where Dascalakis bought his first car, from my grandfather at Ingram Motors.

In the 300 block of South Elm, "Right next to the Princess Cafe was a rooming house (seen here), 24 rooms with 24 baths, all bachelors. No women."

School Spirit

Mary Foust, beloved daughter of UNCG's second president Julius Foust, died giving birth in 1925; one of the magnificent resident halls in the Quad was christened in her honor 3 years later. That's when the unexplained crying noises and other nocturnal anomalies began. Even in recent years there have been reports of footsteps where no person was, horrific shrieks heard only on the third floor... but just below is where most sightings occur.

A spirit haunting Mary Foust would have plenty of company. After hanging herself in the bell tower above Spencer Hall, 'Woman in Blue' Annabelle appears as mist or shadow, hurling objects around, confounding the laws of gravity. Then there's the lonely elderly lady found hanging rope over rafters in her home demolished to make way for Aycock Auditorium. Over the last century she's been spotted more often than an honest politician.

University of North Carolina, Greensboro, N.C.

I Was a Dancing Cigarette Pack in the 50s

Cigarette makers sponsored some of the biggest shows on the (very) small screen in the early days of television, enjoying a close association with America's newest addictive pastime. Aside from whimsical animated 60-second spots often TV ads featured white-coated doctors declaring how healthy their cancer sticks were.

A list of the craziest cigarette commercials of all time would surely include this iconic creation, P. Lorillard Company's dancing cigarette pack of the 1950s.

One of TV's first sensations, an oversized pack of Old Golds with lovely legs prancing aimlessly around in front of a curtain alongside a tiny pack of fast footed matches while the announcer promised a taste, "made by tobacco men, not medicine men." Because if you're going to ingest something into your lungs better it was sanctioned by a North Carolina dirt scratcher than some high falutin' doctor, right?

"My dancing career is so long behind me but the Old Gold commercial keeps coming up in current TV." Jeanne Snow was a hoofer for Lorillard, "I was one of the cigarette packs (with Gloria Vestoff who probably replaced Dixie Dunbar) on Stop the Music with Bert Parks in 1950 & 51—under my maiden name Jeanne Jones (sometimes Jeannie). Harry Salter was the conductor, Jimmy Nygren the choreographer. Other dancers were Louise Ferrand, Bruce Cartwright, and Tom Hansen.

"Incidentally, we were never called the Dancing Butts and, in my tenure, there was no longer a dancing match box."

Old Gold was the leader of the Lorillard brand, in 1956 the tobacco giant opened the world's most modern cigarette factory in Greensboro.

No song and dance
about medical claims...

Old Gold's specialty is to give
you a TREAT instead of a TREATMENT!

Kids, TV & Guns!

Some modern day experts contend that violent video games encourage savage behavior in our young people, while others say that's just another example of the latest entertainment medium becoming society's scapegoat d'jour. Keep in mind, the same breed of expert said the exact same thing about comic books in the '50s and look at how great the baby boomers turned out.

Long before technology gave us realistic video games that allowed kids to simulate predatory gun fighting electronically, America's children took to backyards and playgrounds with toy cap guns to battle it out in the neighborhood. Playing Army and Cowboys and Indians in the dirt was how many American kids spent much of their play time in decades past.

When did this behavior start? Perhaps at the beginning of recorded history, in the 1950s. Cowboys like Roy Rogers, Gene Autry, Hopalong Cassidy,

Advertisers spent over 1.5 billion dollars on TV commercials in 1960.

and The Lone Ranger ruled the daytime TV airwaves, attracting a legion of kids who wanted to play shoot-em-up at home. Not a problem, since all of the television cowboys and detectives had their own line of realistic-looking toy firearms for sale at your nearest dime store. And best of all—no background checks!

The most popular western cap gun sets of the '50s were Mattel's Fanner 50 realistic Winchester rifle, Buc'N Bronco, and the Hubley pistols.

When cowboys and pistol-waving detectives started to lose favor in the early-'60s, toy gun lines lost their key salespersons and innovative products

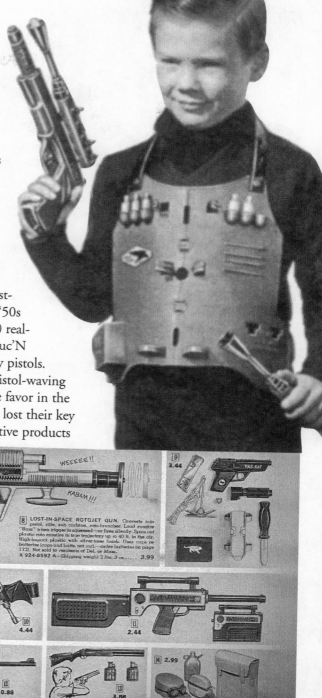

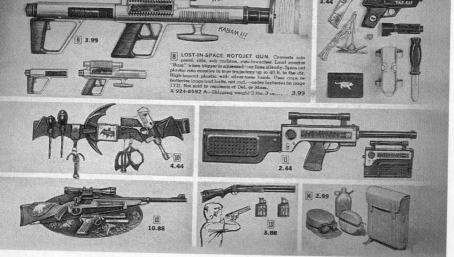

Lost-in-Space Gun

WEEEEE!!

KABAM!!!

8 3.99

8 LOST-IN-SPACE ROTOJET GUN. Converts into pistol, rifle, sub carbine, roto-launcher. Loud rapid-fire "Bam" when trigger is squeezed—or fires silently. Spins out plastic roto-missiles in true trajectory up to 40 ft. in the air. High-impact plastic with silver-tone finish. Uses caps or batteries (caps and batts. not incl.—order batteries on page 172). Not sold to residents of Del. or Mass.
X 924-8592 A—Shipping weight 2 lbs. 3 oz...... 3.99

9 3.44

10 4.44

11 2.44

12 10.88

13 3.88

14 2.99

had to be created from scratch. Products with catchy names like the TommyBurst submachine gun, Remco's Monkey Division (for "jungle warfare" with two-way wrist radios), Secret Sam, and the Fan-O-matic (with Greenie Stick-M caps for ammo) burst on to the market.

Johnny Seven OMA (One Man Army) by Topper was the ultimate killing machine and much sought after—with seven actions, including a grenade launcher, anti-tank weapon, anti-bunker missile, armor piercing shell, and a detachable pistol with the rat-a-tat-tat sound.

"Just position yourself on the hill and attack!" invited the advertising for Johnny Eagle, another of Topper's most popular toy gun lines from the mid-'60s. The brand included the Red River, Mugambo and Lieutenant lines. The ad campaigns flashed iconographic images of kids with their weapons

"I remember when Mattel (I think it was their master stroke) came out with an exact plastic duplicate of that ever-lovin' Vietnamster weapon... the M-16! You cocked it and it fired with a genuine staccato, make believe, 5.56 NATO Commie killing burst!!!!!"

—J. Michael Elliott

drawn, firing down from the hill against a catchy jingle set to the tune of "When Johnny Comes Marching Home." These handsome rifle and pistol sets could be wall mounted on their own simulation wood-grained plaques.

Another highly effective toy campaign was for an all-purpose weapon called Zero-M from Mattel. Who wouldn't want a portable radio or camera that turns into a rapid firing weapon? Sure comes in handy in music class. Back then you didn't expect the electronics to actually work (and they didn't) as long as the gun fired.

In the Zero-M TV commercials, a boy, portrayed by a young Kurt Russell, is summoned by a secret society hidden in his bedroom closet. The old guys in the closet, led by Alfred from the *Batman* series, instruct Kurt to go out into the community armed to the teeth to do their bidding (see also: *Escape From New York*). Needless to say, modern kids would never fall for a setup like that. They don't listen to adults.

Meeting Marion Mack from 'The General'

I met a movie star! Well, I've met lots of stars, this was a silent movie star.

In 1973 Buster Keaton's masterpiece 'The General' was re-released to art houses and was booked at the Janus Theaters a year later. As a teenager I had never seen a Keaton film. My dad talked about enjoying them when he was a kid which prompted me to buy some 8mm shorts; I had experienced those snippets but to see Keaton on the big screen was a surprise and thrill for both my father and myself. (We were back the next weekend when Janus screened W.C. Field's 'The Bank Dick.')

For the 1970s screenings a new print of 'The General' had been struck by Raymond Rohauer who owned the original negative. In the early-1960s he brought Buster Keaton with him to some well-received revival screenings.

Keaton passed away in 1966, for the 1970s revival Rohauer toured with the film's love interest, Marion Mack. This screen gem had been out of the acting side of the business since shortly after Keaton's comedy feature debuted in 1926, pursuing instead a writing career with her husband, B-movie producer Lewis Lewyn. She retired in the 1960s. Not knowing her married name it took Rohauer years to track Marion Mack down.

At that sparsely attended Sunday screening Ms. Mack was as gracious and charming as can be. She seemed to truly relish the praise that came her way for what was a brilliant comedic performance on her part. She shared stories from the set, we were fascinated to hear what the genius Keaton was like in real life, on the biggest production of his career. Wish I could remember a word of it but she was clearly enamored of the man.

'The General' is for many the finest and funniest silent film ever made. If you haven't seen it you should, probably the most accurate representation of the Civil War, near perfect in every sense. It had been a mere 40 years since the actual event.

It may seem odd, given its revered status, but this project destroyed Buster Keaton's career when it flopped at the box office and critics savaged it. As a result, Keaton was never again free to make movies the way he wanted, the results were catastrophic for him and his fans.

Getting Paid to Watch Television in the 1960s

Back in the wild and wooly wilderness days of television, broadcasters were grasping for any gimmick to bring advertisers onboard. As a new, expensive medium they needed to demonstrate an intrinsic value newspapers and radio didn't possess, and those outlets had enjoyed a decades long hold on local businesses. The upstart TV station couldn't reach anyone they didn't already.

Network programs attracting the most viewers were concentrated during nighttime hours, to earn a healthy profit margin stations were left with whatever daytime slots that weren't consumed by soap operas and game shows. That meant scheduling sitcom reruns or creating children's shows that offered advertisers a chance to connect with families in a way radio and print couldn't. Local chat shows were another cheap venue to lure viewers but they were weak tea; there was plenty of talk on the AM dial.

In the mid-sixties a syndicated phenomenon revolutionized the ad biz and proved, once and for all, that video killed the radio star. 'TV Super Bingo' and 'All Star Bingo' offered viewers the thrill of a live game coupled with the biggest stars on television—Agnes Morehead, Ruta Lee, Judy Carne, Stubby Kaye, William Shatner, and other tube faves vying for a national winner that would receive $1000 cash if they were clutching that coveted winning card.

It's where you got the cards that was transformative. By visiting an area grocery chain viewers at home not only had a shot at the big bucks but they could score other cash prizes, up to $100 for one local winner. This was back when $100 was one hundred dollars (around $700 in today's buying power). Shoppers collected as many cards as they could during the week, one at a time, no purchase necessary.

Bingo cards by the thousands flew out of stores, grocers experiencing the power of interactive advertising first hand. Not that radio and print weren't doing basically the same thing, targeted promotions tied to original content, but TV broadcasters were combining must-see television with multi-media branding.

'Off to the Races,' 'Racing Spectacular,' and 'It's Racing Time!' combined the genuine excitement of thoroughbred competition with grocery shopping. If you visited the sponsor that week you had a monied stake in the winners. Didn't score in the first race? Those colorful scratch-off tickets offered 3 chances to prevail on every broadcast. Grand prize for 'It's Racing Time!' was 100,000 Green (or Gold) Stamps to the national weekly winner with a top local cash prize—that magical number, $100.

'Greyhound Derby' was a promotion in the same tradition with championship canines whizzing around a dirt track. Enterprising bargain hunters could, if there were enough participating stores where they lived, spend two hours on a Saturday evening playing Bingo and betting on the dogs and horses. So to speak.

A large tote board in the stores listed winners from the community, often with a polaroid photo next to the lucky person's name. Every once in a while you or someone you knew banked a buck or two. Of course, the actual races had been run long ago, promoters knew exactly how many winning tickets to distribute. Nothing was left to chance.

S&H Green Stamps, TV racing, and Bingo cards—anything to get 'em through the door and in front of the family's new color television set. Along with Roller Derby and Wrestling these half-hours generally aired Saturday evenings around 5:00-7:00pm, dinner hour when folks were most likely to be at home.

These tie-ins were relatively short-lived, people soon tired of the novelty. The payout wasn't worth keeping up with it, regular viewers noticed the same races being run over and over again.

Dialing for Dollars

Many a housewife in the 1960s well into the mid-1970s could be sitting on her couch munching Bon Bons when the phone would ring and a familiar voice was heard to say, "This is Jerry Merritt (or Jo Nelson) from Channel 8's 'Dialing for Dollars' calling. Do you know the count and the amount?" If fair maiden had been watching the morning or afternoon movie she would know that the "count" was the number spun on the wheel early in the program, and the "amount" (what she could win) would be the money accumulated in the pot since the last winner.

'Dialing for Dollars' was based on a national concept, a weekday game played on the air live three or more times during a two-hour motion picture or a block of sitcom reruns. The host would start with an amount of money usually associated with the channel number (channel 8 started with $8.00), each time someone failed to provide the correct answer another $8.00 was added.

Chances of the station actually reaching anyone watching and paying attention was small enough that the jackpot often climbed into the hundreds. Family members would watch the movie just long enough to get the count and the amount (announced during the first commercial break) then post the numbers by the phone, just in case. We know this because it wasn't uncommon for a viewer to quote the numbers from the day before. Ouch. The morning you didn't watch was the day they called.

The New
Andy Griffith
Show

How is it that The Andy Griffith Show has endured on television for more than a half-century? What is it about the notion of a community like Mayberry that continues to resonate with so many Americans? Perhaps it was the level of honesty underneath the necessary artifice. "Everything we said on the show we believed," Andy Griffith declared. "I suppose that's what made it work. We never went for something we didn't believe. It was a good eight years for me, I'll tell you that."

Amateur cartologists place the fictional town of Mayberry about halfway between Greensboro and Raleigh, off I-85 in the great state of North Carolina. But for many modern viewers, Mayberry is less about location and more about what the show represents to them—a way of life that has irrevocably slipped away.

Certainly at the beginning The Andy Griffith Show was a genuinely well-written and superbly crafted show. That's the main reason the program has remained popular, it stands as an idealized snapshot of at least one vision of the American dream. The production of the series coincided with one of the most dramatic cultural upheavals in American history but storylines reflected instead a quaint community where the barber had as much influence as the mayor and the most shocking things that happened was Aunt Bee picketing a construction site or the 'Fun Girls' speeding through the center of town.

The Andy Griffith Show was a spin-off, of sorts. The pilot had been integrated into an episode of The Danny Thomas Show. The executive producer of the series was Richard O. Linke, Griffith's manager. It was producer Aaron Ruben (writer for The Phil Silvers Show), Sheldon Leonard (producer of The Danny Thomas Show) and Andy Griffith's attention to the scripts that made the situations as engaging as they were flat-out funny.

It's no exaggeration to say the nation instantly fell in love with Mayberry's quirky inhabitants, The Andy Griffith Show finished its first season as the number four show in the nation. The lives of Sheriff Andy Taylor (Griffith), his Aunt Bee (Frances Bavier), son Opie (Ron Howard), and deputy Barney Fife (Don Knotts) unfolded in a series of charming, laugh-out-loud episodes that were almost entirely character driven.

Before long, other mildly or wildly eccentric Mayberrians turned up, like Howard McNear who first appeared in episode 13 as befuddled Floyd the barber. "He was just like that," George (Goober) Lindsey once commented about McNear. "I loved working with him. We would come to the studio to watch him work when we weren't working, and that was rare."

Midway through the third season, McNear suffered a massive stroke that paralyzed the left side of his body. He dropped out of the cast but everyone enjoyed working with him so much they arranged for his return in March of 1964. Because of his disability Floyd's scenes had to be shot with the actor sitting down, or leaning against an unseen support.

Jim Nabors joined the show as innocent, dim witted gas jockey Gomer Pyle in January, 1963. Nabor's character was based on his nightclub act where he played the country bumpkin for laughs then sang out in a sublime baritone voice. "I've always liked the character a lot," Nabors said about Gomer. "I've been very blessed to have such a diverse career. I've never been without a job in 40 years."

Gomer was a hit with the public right away, with three catchphrases that lit up the screen in his first year—"Gaaaw-leee," "Shazam," and "Citizen's arrest, citizen's arrest!" After his first few appearances Nabors was so popular he was offered several possible series to star in, including No Time For Sergeants which aired opposite The Andy Griffith Show in the fall of 1964. (Ironically, Griffith and Knotts had starred in the movie, TV special, and stage versions of No Time For Sergeants. Only the weekly TV version didn't have their involvement and it bombed.)

Gomer Pyle, U.S.M.C. was launched in the fall of 1964 and enjoyed a five-year run at the very top of the Neilsens. The pilot episode was produced, written and directed by the fellow who guided The Andy Griffith Show from the beginning, Aaron Ruben.

Beginning of the End

Two major defections meant big changes for year six of The Andy Griffith Show. Aaron Ruben left TAGS to concentrate on Gomer Pyle, U.S.M.C. but he continued to work with Andy and Don. When Griffith, Knotts and Jim Nabors united for a special together in 1965 it was Aaron Ruben they turned to. He also wrote and produced Andy Griffith's Uptown-Downtown Show in 1967 as well as Don Knott's CBS special that year.

In 1965 co-star Don Knotts split from the cast, he was under the impression that Griffith was going to end the series after five seasons so he negotiated a deal with Universal Pictures to star in a series of movies for juvenile audiences. "When Don left after five years I was very nervous," Griffith admitted on reflection in 1968. "There was a lady from TV Guide came in there and she said, 'What are you going to do when Don leaves?' I told 'em not to send her over there. She came anyway. And I didn't feel good that day and I was reading a bad script. And I really didn't have anything to say to her. And she came anyhow, said, 'What are you going to do when Don leaves?' I said, 'I don't know what we're going to do when Don leaves!' And I got up and left and she wrote it just that way. Best article ever written about me. She said, 'he got up and left and didn't even say, 'I appreciate it.'"

Gone as well were the writers who guided the series for those stellar five seasons, guys like Jack Elinson, Harvey Bullock, John Whedon, Michael Morris, Everett Greenbaum and Jim Fritzell (Greenbaum and Fritzell left to write Don Knotts' hit movies The Ghost and Mr. Chicken and The Reluctant Astronaut).

In the fall of 1965, Bob Ross, veteran writer/producer of Amos 'n' Andy and Leave it to Beaver took over as producer of The Andy Griffith Show, broadcast in color for the first time. In a disastrous casting choice (one of many to come), standup comic Jack Burns (of Burns and Schrieber) replaced Don Knotts as Andy's deputy. The fit was not good, resulting in Burn's abrupt departure mid-season.

By default, the focus of the show fell to the remaining supporting players, especially Goober Pyle (George Lindsay) who was introduced as a replacement for his cousin Gomer in 1964. Dour county clerk Howard Sprague (Jack Dodson) joined the regular cast in 1965. These changes seriously affected the quality of the series but there was no noticeable drop in ratings. The Andy Griffith Show was so popular, both as a program and as a notion, that superior scripts were no longer necessary to attract an audience to CBS Monday nights at 9:00. The show was consistently in the top 5—the characters just needed to show up each week and the nation tuned in.

Emment Clark (Paul Hartman) was introduced during the seventh season to replace Floyd in some of the storylines. Too feeble to work any longer, Howard McNear retired at the end of the 1966-67 season. He died two years later.

"We had a great time on the show," George Lindsey stated in 1998. "We respected each other's work so much because everybody was so good. Everybody had their own particular thing they did. Like Howard Morris and like Denver Pyle and then, of course, there's Howard McNear and

Don and Andy and Frances and Anita and the boy, you know the one, the redheaded boy, and Betty Lynn, and all those people."

The show may have crossed over from salty to syrup but the eighth and last season of The Andy Griffith Show brought the highest ratings of the series' run. Both The Andy Griffith Show and Gomer Pyle, U.S.M.C. were riding the very top of the Nielsens for the 1967-68 season, finishing number one and three respectively. Don Knotts won a total of five Emmys for the run of The Andy Griffith Show, two of them after he left as a regular. His eighth season guest shot ('Barney Hosts A Summit Meeting') attracted a 33.4 audience share, making it the most-watched episode of the series' run.

That year, Andy Griffith announced his retirement from weekly TV. Naturally the show's sponsor General Foods didn't want to lose their hold on the number one audience draw in the nation, nor did CBS. It was decided Mayberry would live on—without Andy.

To ease in the transition, in April of 1968 Ken Berry (F-Troop) was introduced as Sam Jones, a gentleman farmer that Andy and Emmett talk into running for the Town Council. Opie Taylor and Sam's son Mike (played by 11-year old Buddy Foster, brother of actress Jodie Foster) were the focus of the next episode. Show 249, entitled Mayberry, R.F.D., established the format (more or less) for the new series and served as the last episode of The Andy Griffith Show.

Same Show New Name

"In Mayberry boys don't wear their hair long. Cut your hair. Period."
—producer Bob Ross to actor Buddy
Foster when he asked if he could grow
his hair out in 1970.

Mayberry R.F.D. (Rural Free Delivery, a postal term for people that lived out in the country) was originally intended to focus on Aunt Bee, the only remaining original cast member to have a regular role on the new series. However, the 65-year old actress was eager to work less, not more. She only appeared in about two-thirds of the episodes during season eight of The Andy Griffith Show and was only pivotal in nine storylines.

If Mayberry R.F.D. was anything, it was evocative and insular. There was no whip behind the cream but before you realized it, you were soaking in it. That's why ratings were exceptional from the very start, there was no serious drop in audience numbers from the last season of The Andy Griffith Show. Mayberry R.F.D. was the second most popular sitcom in the nation in 1968 (Gomer Pyle, U.S.M.C. was first). As with the last three seasons of the Griffith show, former Leave it to Beaver scribe Bob Ross produced.

Exteriors were still being lensed on the Forty Acres set, the backlot built in 1926 for the RKO Studio (later Desilu) where leftover Atlanta sets from Gone With The Wind (those that weren't burned to a cinder) stood-in for the town of Mayberry. In the first episode of R.F.D., Andy Taylor and his girlfriend of four years Helen Crump (Aneta Corsaut) were married and the whole gang turned out for the celebration. This was the only episode of R.F.D. in which Opie Taylor (Ron Howard) and Barney Fife (Don Knotts) appeared. After the wedding, Aunt Bee decides to stay in Mayberry as the Jones' family housekeeper.

Andy turned up briefly in three additional episodes of R.F.D. that first year, after which it was casually explained that he and Helen had moved to Charlotte. The next (and last) time Andy turned up was in an episode during the second season in which he and Helen visit Mayberry with their new baby.

Headmaster Disaster

Despite having left series life behind in 1968, Andy Griffith (a star so big the show he wasn't even on anymore was in the top five) still had a major business interest in television. He owned a significant portion of Mayberry R.F.D., Gomer Pyle, U.S.M.C. and The Andy Griffith Show. (Andy and Gomer continued to be broadcast five times a week on the CBS daytime schedule until 1972.) Andy also had his own line of prepackaged foods being sold in Carolina area grocery stores that included center cut country ham, sausage, pinto beans and black-eyed peas ("with a little more pork and just a pinch of sugar"). He was also a very popular product pusher in television commercials for Jell-O, Kraft Natural Cheese, and Ritz crackers.

Griffith thought 1970 might be a good time to get back into weekly television after his motion picture Angel in my Pocket failed the year before. He enjoyed working with familiar faces so it was only natural that Aaron Ruben would be called in to develop Andy's new show—Headmaster.

With CBS aggressively phasing out their down-home comedies, Andy Griffith understood the need to transition to a younger, hipper audience if he wanted to be a presence on television during the seventies. Griffith's longtime executive producer and manager Richard O. Linke stated: "They signed us for a half-hour weekly series even though we had no script, not even a format in mind. They were willing to take Andy in anything. We could have given them a dirty picture if we wanted to." They should have done that... at least it would have been interesting.

Headmaster debuted in September, 1970, centering around a California coed prep school for teenagers (Concord High School), its dean Andy Thompson (Griffith), his wife Margaret (Claudette Nevins) and the crusty caretaker Mr. Purdy (Parker Fennelly). In a role almost identical to the one he would play eighteen years later on Coach, Jerry Van Dyke (My Mother The Car) was featured as the academy's dorky gym teacher. Van Dyke had previously teamed with Griffith both for his Las Vegas appearances and in Angel in my Pocket.

Unlike The Andy Griffith Show the stories on Headmaster were doggedly serious in nature. In the pilot episode, entitled 'May I Turn You On,' guest-star Butch Patrick (Eddie Munster) was forced to choose between doing drugs or facing the big freeze from all the loadies in his class. On another, Andy dealt with an impending campus riot. It may seem odd in retrospect but this format should have been a surefire recipe for success. 1970-71 was the season when the three networks rolled out show after show with 'Now' and 'Relevant' storylines—The Interns, The Storefront Lawyers, The Young Lawyers, The Senator, The Psychiatrist, and on and on.

The theme song for Headmaster was a folksy tune vocalized by Linda Ronstadt while the overall mood of the production was low key and dull, with just a trace of the folksy sheriff the public had come to know and love. In fact, Andy seemed to have been added as an afterthought in many scripts, there merely to give his sermon on the hot topic of the week. Ron Howard (Opie Taylor) was a guest on one episode and Headmaster was one of Rob Reiner's first writing jobs.

Despite a strong first week sampling Headmaster attracted few viewers to its Friday night timeslot, quickly sinking to number 67 (out of 79 shows). CBS and the star realized the 'relevancy' concept was wrong for Andy Griffith, they were getting creamed by The Partridge Family on ABC. "The man I was playing was of the academic world," Andy said about this unexpected failure. "That is not my world. I was out of my bag. We offered to come up with a whole new show, and (CBS) told us to go ahead."

In November, the network announced the start of production on the program they probably should have put forward in the first place.

The New Andy Griffith Show

Debuting January. 8, 1971, The New Andy Griffith Show was long on Southern hokum but woefully short on laughs. Intentionally, there were few surprises and that was the show's undoing. If Headmaster strained to be relevant, the new Andy show was belligerently irrelevant.

The series was written, created, and produced by Aaron Ruben who guided the first five seasons of The Andy Griffith Show and Gomer Pyle, U.S.M.C. and directed by Lee Phillips, who directed almost all of the last two seasons of TAGS. Earl Hagen crafted the theme song and incidental music to be nearly identical to his efforts for TAGS and Mayberry R.F.D.. This time the setting was an imaginary mid-sized North Carolina town called Greenwood (pop. 12,785, ten times the number of people that lived in Mayberry) with Griffith portraying Andy Sawyer, a returning hometown boy instantly appointed the town's new Mayor Pro-tem.

Andy Sawyer was the model family man, agreeable and understanding, spending lots of quality time with his young 'uns. The kind of dad who takes his eight-year old daughter on a three hour bus ride so he'll have someone to talk to. In other words, no father I ever encountered growing up in the South. In a humble yellow ochre vest, white shirt and gray slacks, Andy Sawyer was more simpleminded and deferential than Sheriff Taylor ever was. Some of his lines would have been more appropriate coming from Goober Pyle.

Lee Meriwether was perfectly cast but under-utilized as Andy's wife. Meriwether was already well-known to TV audiences as a former Miss America who went on to play Catwoman in the Batman movie and Dr. Ann MacGregor on Time Tunnel from 1966-67. More importantly for Griffith, she had been Andy's wife in the motion picture Angel in My Pocket. Marty McCall and Lori Rutherford were seen as the 2.5 kids. Of course, there had to be an older live-in relative—Andy's sister-in-law Nora played by Ann Morgan Guilbert (Millie Helper on The Dick Van Dyke Show and Yetta on The Nanny). Not at all matronly and supportive like Aunt Bee, Nora was constantly complaining, neurotic, meddling, superstitious. A real downer.

Mayberry R.I.P.

For safe measure, The New Andy Griffith Show brought Don Knotts together with George Lindsay as Goober Pyle and Paul Hartman as fix-it man Emmett Clark in a memorable (but confusing) reunion of the former costars, the first in two years. In that episode, Emmett and Goober travel from Mayberry to Greenwood to pressure their old pal Andy to use his influence with the city to rezone a plot of land each of them wants to start a new business.

Strangely, the Mayberry residents don't recognize Don Knotts' unnamed character, even though he's wearing the same salt and pepper suit Barney Fife favored. He wore that very same outfit to Andy and Helen's wedding! Was Barney in the Witness Protection Program?

In the second outing, written by TAGS vets Jim Fritzell and Everett Greenbaum, Glen Campbell was the guest in that old TV chestnut of a plotline—Buff McKnight claims to be friends with Glen Campbell and can get him for the town's centennial show but he doesn't really know Glen so... bet you can guess the rest.

The third episode concerned little old lady Miss Gossagg (played by regular Ruth McDivett) who wants a memorial fountain erected in the town square and insists Andy supervise the project. Besides McDivett, Burt Mustin, Forrest Lewis, Owen Bush, and writer Everett Greenbaum played various townsfolk on both the new and original series.

It was painfully obvious from the start that this production was trying too hard to be The Andy Griffith Show in a larger setting. Scripts were flat and predictable; audiences weren't buying into the derivative premise. Besides, you don't parade around with two different wives in the same season, at least you didn't back then. "Headmaster was a very bad show," Griffith stated in 1971. "And because of Headmaster, The New Andy Griffith Show simply did not have an audience."

Nielsen ratings for the first episode hit number 12 once again then quickly slid back down into the 60s. The series was cancelled on May 21, 1971. Headmaster reruns played out the summer until The New Andy Griffith Show(s) were removed from the schedule. As if that wasn't bad enough, CBS axed the entire town of Mayberry as well—despite Mayberry R.F.D. finishing a solid fifteenth for the final year.

Sheriff Taylor just wasn't needed anymore. Floyd passed away, Barney lived in Raleigh, Opie had grown up, and Aunt Bee moved to Siler City. After eleven years on Monday nights Mayberry itself receded into the past. In a surprise move, CBS cleared the schedule of all of their highly-rated down-home comedies (like Green Acres and Beverly Hillbillies) in the fall of 1971 to make way for shows appealing to more urban viewers, programs like All In The Family, Good Times, Mary Tyler Moore Show, and The New Dick Van Dyke Show.

Aunt Bee's Siler City Cat House

Frances Bavier, Emmy-winning actress who gave life to Aunt Bee on 'The Andy Griffith Show,' was by most accounts the polar opposite of her alter ego. Hardly the domesticated matriarch, Bavier was a sophisticated lady who resided in New York and Los Angeles her entire life, working alongside esteemed actors like Bette Davis and Henry Fonda. A Broadway and motion-picture performer turned small-screen superstar who, in 1970, abruptly decided to walk away from her Top 10 sitcom, 'Mayberry RFD.'

After 15 years of the weekly television-series grind she'd had it with the
Business of Show, one of the reasons why Bavier moved — alone at age 70 — all the way across the continent to Siler City, NC where her biggest fan operated a family furniture store. In this mythical shire mentioned so fondly in scripts produced for her by former writers from 'Amos & Andy' and 'Leave it To Beaver,' she hoped to discover the small-town goodness that she herself had come to represent in the minds of middle America.

Something she clearly had no concept of.

Naturally she was warmly received by Chatham County's 3,700 aw-shucks-just-plain-folks. Grand Marshall in the parades, an honored guest at civic functions, the very flower of verisimilitude as she maneuvered the narrow streets of Siler City in the same pea-green, two-door 1966 Studebaker Daytona she drove on "Mayberry RFD" — now seen five days a week in syndication.

What began as an immersion into Americana quickly disintegrated into what can best be described as an episode of "The Twilight Zone." On Saturday mornings, school buses pulled up in front of her split-level brick home on West Elk Street to unleash the Cub Scouts with instructions to, "Go find your Aunt Bee!" There were neighbors peering through her windows at all hours of the day expecting her to be in character, a role she despised. The few townsfolk she grew close to insisted on calling her "Aunt Bee." Irritating, but she had to have some friends.

In small Southern towns, particularly in that era, if people knew your family you were accepted; newcomers were kept at arm's length. Sure, it's all kissy-kissy, "Can I get you some more sweet tea, Hon?" on the surface but in most folk's minds Miss Bavier would always be that person who moved to town in 1972... from California, no less.

A visit to the town center meant all eyes casting judgment, the ladies at the beauty parlor never forgave her for not joining one of their churches. There were unceasing invitations to Sunday services wherever she went. "Don't forget, you went to church in Mayberry," passers-by would say with a sickly-sweet, curt grin. That was one of Bavier's signature moves on the show!

Week after week the same goobers would bump into her asking, "Was that Opie I saw mowin' yer grass on Sadiddy?" She'd want to scream, "Why are you fixated on my yard?!?" Young couples followed her down the aisles of Byrd's Lo Mark grocery store, "Yer not makin' pickles this summer are ya, Aint Bee?"

Small wonder that, by the 1980s, the former television star was living out of her back bedroom, curtains pulled tight, with 14 devoted kitties for company. She loved her feline companions so much she converted a 250-square-foot bathroom into a sprawling cat box with kitty litter inches deep. What few visitors she had in her final years, store clerks and deliverymen mostly, were overwhelmed by the peeling paint, filthy living conditions and an atmosphere steeped in soft-cream clouds of ammonia that hung over everything like a suffocating umbrella.

Even her "Smart New Look" Studebaker fell prey to the furry Borg; its immaculate vinyl interior shredded, the Chevy 355 cubic inch V-8 engine impossibly clogged with animal dander.

In 1986, three years after she'd stopped venturing out in public, Andy Griffith and Ron Howard made a surprise visit to Siler City's reclusive cat lady. Bavier refused to allow her decade-long coworkers inside, speaking to them only momentarily through the closed front door. This was after declining repeatedly to be part of their Mayberry reunion movie. Why would she participate? She never liked Andy Griffith much from the very beginning.

When she died in 1989, Frances Bavier funneled most of her $700,000 estate into an annuity that, to this day, pays out a yearly Christmas bonus to every Siler City police officer. But her true legacy began gestating not long after she was laid to rest at Oakwood Cemetery. After her home was donated to a local hospital, Bavier's feral cats scampered for the countryside, causing one hell of a population explosion that is only now, a quarter century later, beginning to subside. Ask any Chatham County veterinarian. They are all too familiar with someone bringing in, "One of Aunt Bee's cats."

David Brenner

The sad news came days ago that brilliant comic David Brenner passed away, he was a favorite of Johnny Carson. An amazing storyteller, I remember him mostly from some very funny game show and daytime talk appearances but he was best live on stage with nothing but a spot and a mic.

In the fall of 1977 I was just out of college working as an actor when WTTG's 'Panorama' noontime show announced they were hosting a David Brenner look-a-like contest. People always told me I looked like the comic so what the heck. WTTG was the closest thing to a cable network at that time, one of several superstations (including TBS and WGN) that could be seen in dozens of markets.

'Panorama' was a weekday live talk show with big name guests and musical segments so it had the feel of a laid-back variety show at times. A scaled down 'Merv Griffin Show.' I was booked, David was cohost for the day so there would be a segment where he would interview us. Great exposure. I told all my friends to tune in.

The most exciting part was being in the Green Room with comedy guests Al Franken and Tom Davis, I recognized them from 'Saturday Night Live,' the hottest show on TV in 1977. They were writers and performers from the very beginning. For myself, and every actor I knew, 'SNL' was the dream gig in show business. Franken & Davis peppered me with a few questions, I could tell they were stoned. I guess they thought I was okay so I sat back while they launched into some hilarious shtick with the television set.

We were told David Brenner was running late so musical guests Gotham from New York were given an extra segment then another, they were a high energy band with guitars and horns. Forty-five minutes into the hour-long program the comedian finally made it through the door. That meant no couch time for myself and the other 3 contestants, just a pan across our faces. The winner received tickets for the sold out performance that night at Kennedy Center. It wasn't me. In fact, David said when he came to me, "This guy looks nothing like me." I was just embarrassed that I told my friends to watch.

David pulled us aside after the broadcast, apologized profusely, then called over his business manager to have him add our names to the guest list. This Carolina boy had never been on a big-time guest list before.

Lacking anything else to do I drove over to Kennedy Center a couple of hours early, have a look around, take in the beautiful surroundings. Not at all by accident I found myself on the stage that was set up for the comedian with a single microphone, front and center. A single work light was on near the back wall and the house lights were up. I approached the microphone, stared out across that magnificent theater, standing where legends of show business stood, feeling so big and so small at the same time.

Walking off to cheers of 'Encore! Encore!' from the packed house in my mind a stagehand stopped me—momentarily. "Oh, sorry Mr. Brenner, go right ahead." I did, right into the dressing room. Deluxe.

When it came time to take our seats I was approached by a number of people who recognized me from the telecast earlier that day, from just those few quick shots. That was eye opening. As was the flash mob that surrounded me when someone in the lobby yelled, "I saw you on TV today!" Frightening.

In that brief exchange with David Brenner it was easy to see what a nice guy he was, and this was the peak of his career. Thanks for the tickets.

After You've Gone

When Judy Garland brought her bombastic musical review to War Memorial Auditorium on April 17, 1961 there was no way of knowing a week later she'd be making the biggest comeback ever by staging what would be dubbed, "the greatest night in show business history." Greensboro was her last stop before playing a sold-out Carnegie Hall on April 23rd to the grandest ovation and display of adulation a star has ever known. A year and a half earlier, with an inflamed liver, Garland was told by doctors she'd live the rest of her life as a semi-invalid and never work again. The 38-year old was considered washed up by Hollywood and the music industry.

Some among the 2,400 attendees were perturbed that the venue was switched last minute from the coliseum to the smaller auditorium but, because of the overflow, 240 lucky concert goers got to watch from the orchestra pit. Ticket prices ranged from $2.00 to a high of $4.50. Greensboro was the conclusion of a grueling tour. Miss Garland's throat was hoarse, she was a bit plump but accustomed to performing under harsh conditions, why Mel Tormé nicknamed her "The Concrete Canary."

Her performance the next week in New York was so electrifying it became a bellwether against which every other entertainer is measured. The sound-track album won 4 Grammy Awards, the first double LP to go Gold after 13 weeks at #1.

Last of the Drug Store Lunch Counters

In the 1940s-1970s virtually every drug and variety store had their own lunch counters. Woolworths downtown stopped serving food in 1993, then closed altogether a year later. Rumor has it 'The Black Widow' Blanche Taylor Moore toasted sandwiches at the Eckerds on Yanceyville Road. Considering she sprinkled arsenic like MSG at a fast food buffet... I'd avoid the chicken salad sandwich.

Kinard Drug on the corner of Battleground and Cone was popular with both Grimsley and Page students in the 1970s. In the 1980s in-store lunch counters vanished leaving only one in Greensboro, located inside Brown-Gardiner on Elm Street. In fact, it's expanded its footprint over the years. My aunt Gertrude Tankersley worked the front register in the 1960s & 1970s.

The Old Rebel

Whatever Happened to the Old Rebel?

In 1950, a year after WFMY first took to the airwaves and five years before Captain Kangaroo unlocked the doors to his Treasure House, an unknown performer named George Perry debuted on "Six-Gun Playhouse," a live children's program featuring clown acts, western serials and black-and-white cartoons. After a short period, Perry dropped the cowboy persona to don a black top hat, frock coat and old-fashioned bow tie to become the Old Rebel, one of the most beloved characters ever to parade across our screens.

Local kid shows were all the rage on TV in the 1950s; just set the cameras up and let the talent fill time with whatever they came up with. This unexplored electronic environment was ideal for George Perry, with his limitless

imagination and singular ability to make his young audience believe wholeheartedly in whatever whimsical notion he was trying to convey.

"The Old Rebel Show was a work of love for my dad and plenty of fun too." George's son Timm Perry told me, "The main philosophy was to 'entertain, enlighten and educate.' My father was a native of Statesville, survived bullets, bombs and fire during World War II's Battle of the Bulge and, after the war, toured Europe with an acting troupe. When he returned to North Carolina, he was an announcer in the Statesville and Asheboro radio markets before being hired by WFMY in 1950 where he was a commercial announcer, part-time weatherman, built sets, served as cameraman and film engineer among other duties until he took over as the Old Rebel.

"Hundreds of thousands of youngsters appeared on the 'magic moving playhouse' bleachers and scores celebrated their birthdays in the studios. Coca-Cola and Dr. Pepper were early sponsors so drinks were wheeled into the studio by the crateful atop shopping carts to give to the kids in the audience. My mother also joined in the festivities by cooking dozens of Curtis hot dogs and serving them on delicious Holsum bread rolls. Many people don't know that my father carved the show's puppets himself."

In the early fifties it was far from certain that television was going to catch on with the public. TV sets were massively expensive (more than $1,500 in today's money), screens were miniscule, reception was deplorable and precious little content was available to fill the hours. It wasn't until children's programs like 'Howdy Doody' nationally and The Old Rebel Show locally began attracting youngsters that the TV tide started to turn. It became a race to "keep up with the Joneses" once dad witnessed his offspring running over to the neighbor's house to watch television... and nothing sold television receivers like putting a family's precious tykes on the screen.

Triad viewer Marsha Peele remembers, "As a young girl growing up in Greensboro during the 1950s, I, like all the kids I knew, had our favorite heroes. The Old Rebel, Lone Ranger and Superman were our heroes. Unlike the other guys, Old Rebel was attainable. I never will forget one day I was waiting to visit my dentist, Dr. Kilkelly, and none too happy about the upcoming regular exam. It was a small office and the doctor had just let out his last patient and was leading me into the examination room. Suddenly, the hall door opened

The
OLD REBEL
PECOS PETE SHOW
Monday thru Friday
5 pm·

and in rushed the Old Rebel... in full costume! I was aghast! My mouth literally fell open.

"He apologized for the interruption and asked the doctor to see him immediately as it was something of an emergency and he was due for an appearance somewhere. I gladly gave my hero my dentists' chair... after all this was little enough to do for one's hero. On his way out, he shook my hand and thanked me profusely. It was the best visit to a dentist I have ever had!"

In 1953 Jim Tucker joined the show as a friendly cowboy character; there-after the broadcast became known as The Old Rebel and Pecos Pete Show. Joining them was a pug-nosed pooch appropriately named Troubles, and Cathy the Chimp. Having a chimpanzee as a regular was not that unusual in the fifties but Troubles was forced to drop out in the early sixties after biting down on one too many of the small hands he was supposed to lick.

Timm Perry got to know Jim Tucker, "Jim as Pecos Pete was a great cowboy, easygoing and kindly, a congenial co-host with a wide range of talents from the Wild West trail, including rope trick artistry, sharp-shooting and melodious guitar picking. Rebel and Pecos made countless appearances over a three-state area; they interviewed big western stars like Gene Autry and Dennis Weaver and ventured backstage at Greensboro's National Theatre in the fifties to flirt with the pretty Carter Sisters [June later married Johnny Cash] where a bashful fellow introduced himself to them... it was Elvis Presley!"

Lee Marshall began appearing regularly around 1962 as Lonesome Lee the Clown and remained with the program until the very last episode, bringing with him a bizarre cast of characters that included Chee-Chee, a talkative worm in an apple, and Johnny Lee, his whacked-out ventriloquist dummy.

Mike Marshall recalls, "My father, Lee Marshall, did a lot of clowning including working with Ringling Brothers and was a fixture in Piedmont Christmas parades, company parties, children's parties and similar events. I sometimes accompanied him to WFMY where my dad would join George Perry and the others in the dressing room before the show to get ready. Most of the time there was no script... George, my dad, or one of the other characters would have some simple idea and they would kick it around as they put on their costumes and makeup and basically ad-lib on the air.

"When I went off to college in 1963 (UNC Chapel Hill), the show came on at five in the afternoon. I lived in a dorm and would sometime go down to the TV room to watch it, that is until another student would show up and ask, 'Are you really watching that kid show?' Of course, I'd yield the TV and walk away."

By 1964, the Triad's leading kids' show boasted an extraordinary 15,000 members of the Old Rebel and Pecos Pete Club - to whom the station mailed out packages stuffed with club pins, a song sheet, secret decoder and a photo album.

Besides the Old Rebel, Pecos Pete, and Lonesome Lee other occasional cast members included Coocoo the Clown, ventriloquist Ted Moss and his pal Hal, Tiny the Clown and his trained K-9 Hot Dog, and "Uncle" Roy Griffin (executive director of the Greensboro Community Center) who popped in every few weeks to teach lessons in civic responsibility. There were also filmed cartoon features including characters like Popeye, Wally Gator, Touch Turtle, Lippy the Lion and Space Angel.

John Hitchcock was on the show once, "Remember, this was before cable. We could only get three TV stations with rabbit ears—channel 2 (about 2-3 miles away), channel 8 (pretty good reception), and 12 (barely could see it through the 'Snow'). If you were in Greensboro, you watched WFMY-2, period.

"I was at the top of the bleachers, we were jammed in like mackerels and after a six-ounce Coke I got sick and threw up. I'm sure that made a lasting impression at Channel 2."

At a time when racial tensions were high you would think a show with the word "Rebel" in the title might be problematic given the Old South implications. Instead, The Old Rebel Show was a place where kids of all colors congregated and nobody thought that much about it. Early on George Perry saw the need to fill the studio bleachers with kids from across the spectrum and would often drive out himself to pick up youngsters at the Hayes-Taylor YMCA to make sure all local children were consistently represented.

Riding the Baby Boom shockwave with ratings at an all-time high, the show's stars were in high demand for personal appearances, parades, shopping center promotions, private birthday parties and charity benefits.

John Hitchcock recalls a local holiday tradition, "The downtown Christmas Parade in Greensboro was the big-time. One year there was Uncle Roy in an antique car, Lonesome Lee walking his invisible dog on a leash, Bob Gordon from Channel 12's Sunday afternoon show, local news and weather folks (good 'ole Lee Kinard and Charley Harville), and the master of ceremonies - the Old Rebel - riding on a vintage fire truck along with his mute polar bear, Marco.

"From the front steps of Millie Hopkins' nursery school, that's as close to heaven as a kid gets. Well, I could have caught a miniature loaf of bread from Little Miss Sunbeam, but you can't have it all."

1967-1977

It was the top story on the playground in the summer of 1967, an event of seismic proportions... Pecos Pete was leaving The Old Rebel Show. After 14 years, the Old Rebel & Pecos Pete had become synonymous; the playful camaraderie they exhibited on camera was something that couldn't be recreated.

Jim Tucker left to join the on-air staff at WSJS Channel 12 (now WXII) as co-host of their morning program Today at Home. The Old Rebel Show was moved to mornings eventually settling in at 9 a.m. which meant George Perry and the former Pecos Pete were directly competing with each other for

viewers (up against WGHP's Dialing For Dollars). Today at Home ran for four years.

Jim Wiglesworth joined The Old Rebel Show in 1968 as Jungle Jim to replace George Leh, a remarkably talented puppeteer who, from the very beginning, provided the homespun personalities for Homer the Hound and Marvin the Mule. Wiglesworth brought with him a youthful exuberance and inventive wit; he also began utilizing blue screen and other cutting edge color videotape technology to give The Old Rebel Show a more modern feel.

"I remember sitting down one day with George Perry and telling him I would love to fill in and try to develop these puppets. He quickly agreed, 'Why not give it a shot?' Marvin the Mule went into retirement and Homer the Hound forever after became known as Mr. Wiglesworth. I created several more puppet characters, there was Humphrey, a grumpy ole character who pretended to hate kids and love pickles; later came Charlie, a more mellow character who played well off of Humphrey.

"Every day we always had the kids in the audience walk through the door on the set and give us their names. If it was a smaller group, often the Old Rebel would ask questions like what school or what town were they from. We had kids from southern Virginia to just outside of Charlotte and everywhere in between. We also had a daily 'Birthday Spotlight.' Children from all over the state (as well as Virginia, it seemed) would send in their pictures. I can't even guess how many thousands of those we showed over the years.

Jim Wiglesworth, "I did receive a little compensation for doing this show but I did The Old Rebel Show for all those years because I liked doing it. I liked the purpose, making kids happy (man, does this sound sappy... but it's true). I was a full-time producer/director for the station and my

Joan Crawford and The Old Rebel were both big supporters of the Muscular Dystrophy Association. Remember the backyard carnival kits?

responsibilities were to write and produce television commercials and direct the 11 O'Clock news. From the station's standpoint, my relationship with George and The Old Rebel Show was my own personal labor of love.

"Possibly the worst golfer I've ever known, George truly loved the sport. He and I and his son Timm played golf on a fairly regular basis."

Melinda Wrenn Thomas was another avid watcher, "I remember a special day. A special day especially if you lived in or around Greensboro. It was my fifth birthday party. I was so excited because my friends and I were going to be on The Old Rebel Show. At first the butterflies were too intense because I was going to meet Old Rebel himself, walk through that familiar door and shake the hand of someone I watched with great anticipation. I remember sitting on those cold bleachers sipping on a Pepsi and watching Lonesome Lee entertain us with his worm sliding in and out of his big red apple. I felt so big and so loved at the same time. I knew I was with someone who cared for me and all my friends with me that day.

"After introductions our main role as audience members was to cheer for the skits and finally wave to the audience at home as the cameras panned across each kid's face on the bleachers. We were given Coca-Colas from small green glass bottles and those little orange peanut butter crackers - after that we went absolutely wild with sugar and caffeine!

James Counts grew up in Thomasville, "I was surprised to be able to watch myself on the show a couple of days later, that it was recorded and not live. I was also amazed that on one show the Old Rebel took his grey top hat and painted it cherry red, trading his grey vest for a matching red one. Unlike many sitcoms and cartoons I watched at the time, this change was permanent and he never wore the grey outfit again."

Several times WFMY dropped hints that it might cancel The Old Rebel Show but the outcry from the public was tremendous, so in 1976 they bumped the program to Saturday mornings at 7, now expanded to an hour.

During the summer of 1977, I was on a promotional tour for the Land of Oz theme park in Boone and one of our stops was The Old Rebel Show, which taped on a Friday afternoon. This was one of the last programs, there was no longer a studio audience full of excitable kids and George Perry and Lonesome Lee seemed to know that the writing was on the wall. We clowned around with the Old Rebel, he developed a "crush" on Dorothy, the puppets came out from behind the curtains and a fine time was had by all.

That summer we attended numerous charity events across the state and at every function there was the Old Rebel. He was tireless in his devotion to muscular dystrophy in particular (remember his MDA backyard carnival kits?) and worked so hard to entertain those severely disabled kids. And they were a tough audience, let me tell you.

Jim Wiglesworth, "I left The Old Rebel Show in March or April of 1977. I heard through the grapevine later that summer WFMY was thinking of canceling George's show come fall. I remember going over one day and sitting in the office of Chuck Whitehurst, the station's general manager at the time, and pleading with him not to cancel this show. His major reason for this decision was that, with all the federal regulations pertaining to advertising certain products targeted at children, he did not want to mess with it.

"I tried with all my powers to get him to see that it just didn't matter if this program generated a single penny in direct revenue, it was worth it (and then some) in public relations and good will. But he was the boss and I no longer worked there—so guess who won that debate.

After his show was cancelled, George Perry took up reporting occasional folksy, human-interest stories on the Channel 2 news and was pretty good at it but he was dropped unceremoniously after a few months, fired by what one WFMY employee referred to as, "a vengeful general manager."

Jim Longworth, host of Triad Today, worked at WFMY, "Of course the sad thing about The Old Rebel Show was the way it was phased out. Management determined that the show needed to go because it was not profitable. The truth is, it was never a profit center; it was an audience builder and image builder for WFMY. High above the studio was a huge observation room that could hold hundreds of moms, dads, grandparents and friends of the kids who came to tape the show each afternoon.

"We usually had about eighty to a hundred kids in the bleachers and a hundred or more spectators. Those folks went home all excited and told their friends and family about The Old Rebel Show, creating tremendous goodwill and word of mouth. It was, in a sense, that goodwill that built the

station's ratings and enabled the sales department to sell spots at a premium rate for the 6 p.m. and 11 p.m. news.

"George Perry was a great broadcaster committed to providing quality local programs to his audience. Were he alive today, he would be hurt to know that none of our TV stations have continued with the work he started. Shame on us for abdicating our responsibility to children in favor of syndicated programming. Television airwaves belong to the public, so TV should be about public service not just profits. Perhaps the Old Rebel will be reincarnated as a TV station manager and he will resurrect the local kid's show. We can only hope."

In 1978, Old Rebel turned up with Bob Poole on a Saturday morning radio show for WBIG-AM, airing live from the K&W Cafeteria inside the struggling Carolina Circle Mall. Neither of these media giants was terribly comfortable in this format. Bob Poole, the Triad's undisputed morning radio king for three decades, was in ill health and suddenly working with a live audience while the Old Rebel, fully decked out in his familiar outfit, was a TV children's host facing a room full of old folks wolfing down free biscuits and gravy. The program had a short run; Bob Poole passed away not long after.

Later that year George Perry was spotted at the unemployment office in Greensboro. Taunted by teenagers who easily recognized the pipe-smoking TV star, he left without being able to transact his business. How humiliating that must have been for this 30-year veteran in broadcasting, arguably the most recognizable personality in the area, one of a handful of people (along with Charlie Harville and Lee Kinard) who transformed WFMY from an iffy proposition into a multi-million dollar business.

George Perry died of a heart attack in 1980 at age 59, just three years after losing his job. Doctors may have labeled it a cardiac arrest but there's no doubt that not being able to do what he loved most is what broke his heart.

Timm Perry, "Throughout the years my dad led a creative, productive life. He married a beautiful redhead named Martha, painted outstanding artworks, carved figurines and puppets out of wood, wrote poetry, played banjo and tenor guitar, raised vegetables and flowers, read biographies and history voraciously, fished, golfed and hosted WFMY's RFD Piedmont. I loved the guy. Everybody loved the guy. You would have loved him too if you had known him!"

Old Rebel Show Reunion

In 2000, I put on an Old Rebel Show reunion with the help of the Greensboro Public Library's children's curator James Young, who holds the distinction of being one of the kids bitten by Troubles, the show's canine mascot.

Lonesome Lee Marshall and Jim Wiglesworth were there along with George Perry's widow Martha Perry, Timm Perry and family members of Jim (Pecos Pete) Tucker. Tucker, who left WSJS in the mid-1970s to open a Baskin-Robbins in the new Hanes Mall, was ill at the time of the reunion and joined that great roundup in the sky soon after.

We didn't know what to expect or even if anyone would show up; the program had been off the air for more than 20 years but the crowd, who came from as far as Raleigh, was wildly enthusiastic. Parents who grew up with the Old Rebel brought their youngsters who laughed uproariously at clips from the show. These modern preschoolers reacted just as we did at their age, loving every minute of it. There's something timeless in what George Perry and his co-stars brought to the small screen, an incandescent charm that transcended generations.

Co-star Jim Wiglesworth thinks we've lost something, "I do feel there is something very nice and friendly about a local show of this type. The nature of the beast, 'broadcasting,' has changed so much in recent years that local stations can easily and cheaply buy a packaged program from a syndicator rather than create one themselves. Unfortunately, they don't have a local flavor and children today don't seem to have any more loyalty to one station than to any other. Children can't go visit and they don't have any local heroes."

(Lonesome) Lee Marshall passed away July 3, 2004 at the age of 89. Today, "Jungle" Jim Wiglesworth is a successful real estate agent in Greensboro and the father of first season Survivor runner-up Kelly Wiglesworth. He was also the first to license Winston Cup Racing for TV broadcast, now known as NASCAR. Timm Perry carries on the family tradition of entertaining children, he's in much demand especially during the holidays. It's amazing how much he sounds like the Old Rebel.

No question, television stations lost a key connection to the community they serve with the demise of locally produced children's shows. Oh sure, WFMY or WGHP will occasionally invite a group of youngsters into the studio to watch a news broadcast but somehow children sitting through stories of home invasions, murder and other assorted deviant activity doesn't exactly substitute for the character-building skits or lessons in manners that were offered up daily from those very same studios 30 or 40 years ago.

Like it or not, life in front of the tube will never be the way it was during television's messy adolescence. For my generation and the one that came before and after, George Perry remains nothing less than an icon, a remarkably positive influence on our psyches, a lasting spirit in the community and symbol of a way of life that we can romanticize now that it's rooted firmly in the past, never to return.

Martha and Timm Perry passed away in 2010 & 2011.

In 1968 Channel 48 signed on the air at 3:30 in the afternoon with a local show, The Kiddie Scene with Mr. Green. I was on that program as a youngster, using a parody of Dragnet from Cracked magazine as a script I wrangled kids in the neighborhood to put on a play in the back yard of 1200 Hill Street. For whatever reason, I called Channel 48 and asked if we could perform the skit on their daytime kid's show and they said yes.

My dad drove us down to the station, one of the few times I remember him taking us anywhere. During the taping my younger brother, who was in the first grade, missed his cue so one of the girls in the skit called him a "dumbass." That had to be edited. This was a real 'Little Rascals put on a play' event. The only other thing I remember about the program was that they played Yakety Sax and Charlie Brown constantly.

At that time, WUBC channel 48 was a small, independent station in the warehouse district of Greensboro, located on Wendover Avenue (I think) offering B movies, a dance show that followed Kiddie Scene called The Now Generation, public affairs shows like Questions, Answers, Opinions and reruns of The Outer Limits, Patty Duke and Route 66. They also aired syndicated country western shows like Stone & Atkins, Roller Derby, as well as The Steve Allen Show weeknights.

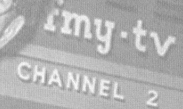

Tune to the
OLD REBEL AND PECOS PETE SHOW
for the code ciphers to use with the
MAGIC WHEEL CODE CARD

Decode the mystery message. Then send to the Old Rebel and Pecos Pete Club, WFMY-TV, Greensboro, N. C.

Outer circle for the first of the code ciphers

Visit 'The Old Rebel' tribute site for rare video & more: TVparty.com/oldrebel.

Uncle Roy

Pat McCrory vs the Hippies

Outwardly conservative, Catawba College in the mid-1970s was a full-on party school—toga parties, Purple Jesus parties, alcohol fueled panty raids, $2.75 all you can drink night at the Buckaneer Lounge. The campus paper was crowded with ads for Old Milwaukee, Schlitz Malt Liquor, and Wild Irish Rose fortified wine. Debates raged over whether students would attend a school sponsored dance if alcohol wasn't served. They wouldn't.

There were so many drunken soirees the jocks and business majors (one and the same at that time) failed to run for office or show up to vote in the 1976-77 elections, resulting in a Student Government Association overwhelmed by feminists and long-haired, peace-and-love types. SGA President Frank Mianzo was a hippie right out of Central Casting; with stringy, below the shoulder black hair and a full beard he could have easily passed for one of the Fabulous Furry Freak Brothers. He adopted a laissez-faire approach to enforcing the more archaic rules governing campus life. Students hauled before the Judicial Court for public intoxication or dorm visitation violations were most likely let off with a warning, as opposed to the overly harsh sentences common in years past.

School beautification was Mianzo's focus, he organized a campus work day that saw half the student body landscaping and washing away the purple pools of puke that flowered outside the dorms. He struck out for more transparency in student government, advocated for women and minority issues, and booked concerts by Doc & Merle Watson, folk singer Tom Chapin, and Pure Prairie League.

You can almost smell the patchouli from here.

Many on campus feared,

without a course correction, Catawba College was on the verge of becoming a hippie enclave. The more conservative students, practically everyone who wasn't in the drama or music departments, were especially alarmed over this development.

Who better to turn back the liberal tide than political science major Pat McCrory, the only arch-conservative serving on the senate that year. As leading member of the Grievance Committee his focus up to then had been on getting the clocks synchronized on campus. And you know who else synchronized the clocks, don't you?

McCrory mounted an aggressive campaign for SGA President in 1977 in a effort to return student government to the strident old-boy's-club it had been throughout the 1960s and early 1970s, when campus protests raged absolutely nowhere near Salisbury, NC. He and others encouraged jocks from the business, accounting, and economics departments to campaign for office. They flooded the ticket. McCrory's opponent, James Shriver, was himself a business major with Bama Bangs and a winning personality.

As someone who attended Catawba during those years I personally liked Pat, he had a brash confidence I had to admire. I'd never met the guy when he rang me up freshman year, after finding my name and address in the student directory, to ask if I could give him a ride home to Greensboro the next time I was going. That happened a few times, I can't recall what we talked about during the 45 minute drives but it was clear we had little in common other than our similar upbringings. He was class president in high school, I was class clown. As far as I could tell he was a straight up guy; stubbornly square and proudly so.

Then there was that damn smile of his. What the fuck was he so happy about all the time—being one of the best looking guys around, popular and athletic? Maybe the sun was in his eyes, I don't know, it was unnerving. I had to wonder at times if there was anything of substance behind that cheshire grin.

During 'The Great Debate' (that's what they called it) between the presidential candidates McCrory stood steadfastly against a proposed $2.87 rise in fees, most of it to be directed toward the struggling student publications. Due to "wasteful spending" he wanted budgetary oversight across the board, especially over the newspaper and arts magazines, and promised a more forceful approach to student discipline.

This stood in contrast to James Shriver who didn't share Pat's zeal for budget cutting and supported a more lax enforcement of visitation hours. He planned to continue many of the course corrections enacted under Frank Mianzo's term in office, expressing a desire to work closely with the outgoing President (voted most popular guy on campus that month) and with the heads of all departments.

A get out the vote campaign assured conservatives of a clean sweep and that's just what happened. But McCrory's coup happened without Pat, when the votes were tabulated on April 14, 1977 his reputation as a scold doomed him. In a surprise upset the mellower candidate, with no previous political experience, prevailed.

McCrory obviously learned from this experience when he ran for Governor of North Carolina in 2011, waging a substance free campaign by not expressing his more controversial views or intentions in public— thereby coasting to victory on a Koch and a smile.

Stone Arches on Spring Garden in Lindley Park

These monuments, recently restored, are believed to have once served as the gateway to an amusement park in the 1800s.

May All Your Stoplights Be Green

Bob Gordon Popcorn Theater enjoyed a decade long run beginning in 1966 with Robert Van Horn (Bob's real name) VJ-ing for an entertainment starved audience. Earlier in the decade the easy-going emcee presented cartoons weekday afternoons then headed up The Bob Gordon Show outfitted in the manner of a gentleman cowboy, six shooters on each hip, to entertain youngsters in the mornings. Like other kiddie stars Bob had his own secret code and hosted animal acts but one feature wasn't at all typical, calling viewers on the air that sent in their crayoned drawings and phone numbers.

In 1966 Bob moved over to Saturday and/or Sunday afternoons for a video hodgepodge of reruns, movies, and 1940's serials. Bob Gordon Theater (the Popcorn came and went) varied in length and schedule, 3-4 hours (more or less) getting underway around 1:00 or 2:00, a casual affair remembered

Monkey likes cotton candy! David Dry took this photo at the Dixie Classic Fair in the early 60's.

mostly for the dollar bills Bob origamied into exotic shapes and amusing banter with his ventriloquist dummy Van, a holdover from the children's program.

Obviously a degree of consideration was given to the show's balanced menu, a video salad bar for TV junkies young and old. Well-written sitcoms, fanciful dramas, westerns, and kid's standards tossed into an unlikely mix—The Many Loves of Dobie Gillis, Adventures of Superman, Bus Stop, McHale's Navy, Cheyenne, and Bachelor Father were in rotation in the late 1960s alongside a chapter or two of Buck Rogers or Zombies of the Stratosphere. A common thread? All enjoyable entertainment even if you weren't into that genre.

Frustrated today with hundreds of channels yet nothing worth watch? Imagine a mere 3 TV outlets airing little more than church services, religious pseudo-dramas, country music jamborees, and staged nature programs on the weekends. Before WSJS (now WXII) beamed Bob Gordon Theater into our Philcos anything more exciting than Davey & Goliath was likely achieved by crimping tin foil to rabbit ears in an attempt to hone in on an affiliate in Raleigh or Charlotte where you might discover, at best, an episode of I've Got A Secret buried inside a blizzard of static.

Sandwiched between the reruns were live segments with Bob sharing behind-the-scenes stories about what was coming up next, showcasing area talent, or interacting with ordinary people with interesting hobbies. One guest made an impression on me, collector Clay Kimball who brought with him rare comic books that probably lost half their value after Bob flung them around like last week's TV Guide. That appearance was in conjunction with the Greensboro Public Library where a few dozen four-color rarities were enshrined under glass-and-key for us supergeeks to marvel over... and some unknown thief to make off with.

Bob was very creative with his hands, every Christmas instructing viewers on how to construct a Moravian Star. Martin Kirby was a fan, "Bob Gordon Theater was a favorite of mine as a child. I loved the westerns but most of all it was fun to watch Bob try his paper folding skills. So many times they just didn't work but he had another one to the side that had worked earlier. It was great fun. They don't make'm like that anymore."

In 1969 Bob presided over the first WSJS Halloween Spooktacular, a block of 4 classic Universal horror films broadcast primetime into the late hours. Bob Gordon Theater's bounty of escapism in the early seventies leaned more towards action and sci-fi with Rat Patrol, 77 Sunset Strip, Sugarfoot, Secret Agent, One Step Beyond, The Invaders, and Time Tunnel.

As the decade progressed NBC Sports took on a more aggressive stance resulting in Bob Gordon Theater being sidelined for weeks at a time, sometimes only filling an hour or less, before disappearing altogether in 1977. By then Bob was hosting Daybreak, a half-hour talk show airing early weekday mornings. He's long been retired and lives with his wife in Winston Salem.

Booked as a guest on the WXII Channel 12 morning show in 2003 I brought along my Bob Gordon Show Fan Club card. No one on set knew anything about it, I didn't expect them to, but they displayed the card full screen to open the interview. I secretly hoped Robert Van Horn might see it, recognize a hat tip to the man who exemplified a generation of television broadcasters perfectly at ease lounging in front of a live camera with an unscripted 5 minutes to kill, a personality filling the screen without ego or artifice.

Not As Easy as ABC

In 1908 North Carolina became the first Southern state to prohibit the sale or consumption of "intoxicating spirits." In 1920 if you wanted to score booze you casually ambled behind where Elon University School of Law is now to purchase a bushel of apples with a Mason jar of white lightnin' concealed within. More upstanding citizens could score bottled and bonded liquor at the Old Express Office—wink wink, nudge nudge. Fordham's Drug Store also stocked illegal hootch but if the liquid in the two large glass globes in the front windows was colored red it meant the revenuer was around. Come back again when the water turns green.

Long Gone Fast Food Joints

A flood of fast food chains in the late-fifties and early-sixties, many long forgotten, washed away virtually every ma and pa diner in their wake. Boomers, the first generation to find it perfectly acceptable that a clown would represent an eating establishment, can look back nostalgically on a time when fast food was of a much higher quality. I'm still miffed about McDonald's french fries being nothing like the limp, greasy ones of my youth, so irresistible because they were sizzled in beef fat. Modern day outlets like KFC serve a product nothing like what they offered a few decades ago, menus today are geared for even the dullest employee to execute.

Where can you get that retro 1970's taste experience today without programming the Time Tunnel? (A risky proposition considering the Tunnel exploded into a shower of sparks whenever someone moved a dial.) It is possible, depending on where you are, to travel back to the past—gastronomically speaking.

Biff Burger

In the seventies there were several Biff Burger restaurants around town, they were located all along the east coast with a few outposts not too much further west. In the quality pecking order of burger chains there was McDonald's at the top, Burger King just below, Hardees, Burger Chef, with Biff Burger bringing up the rear. Their standard hamburger differed from the competition thanks to a proprietary tangy sauce the patty was dipped into after roasting in a special rotating broiler.

In the days of 20 cent burgers, Biff ("Best in Fast Food") cost only 19. Being less expensive than the

A 1960s Winston-Salem Biff Burger.

other chains led to the impression, in my mind, that the burgers weren't as good—indeed, they had a slightly gamey taste. The chain was founded in the 1950s but went under in the mid-1970s with a number of profitable independents holding on. Biff Burger disappeared almost entirely in the mid-1980s but two stores survive still using the original recipes and the same basic decor. One is in St. Petersburg, Florida. The other was rechristened Beef Burger, a 50+ year Greensboro institution with the 1970's chairs and tables (yellow and attached as one unit, naturally) along with a collection of 1980's arcade games.

Still utilizing the classic "Biff" character, one of the worst designed mascots in history, they churn milkshakes from a 1970's machine and the food is grease-liscious. I'm not crazy about the Biff Burger itself but they have the best steak sandwich I've had for the price. UNC-G students have long flocked here to chow down on cheap but good quality eats that really soak up the alcohol—even though the front door sports a sign reading, "If you're drunk eat somewhere else." That's half your clientele! Sadly, Lee Street expansion plans by the college threatens the future of Beef Burger, hopefully it can be assimilated into UNC-BORG as Yum Yum and Old Town Draught House were.

Burger Chef

Another lost burger chain selling down-market sandwiches that I liked just fine. Their commercials attempted to tap into the teen market with groovy hippie music and tender but occasionally offbeat family images. "Incrediburgable!" Burger Chef's demise coincided with Wendy's going nationwide in the early-seventies, pushing the fast food palate in a new direction with their salad bar, fresher meat, and innovative drive-thru window. The operation began to vanish in the mid-eighties after Hardees bought them out, the last Burger Chef was shuttered in 1996. The big two—McDonald's and Burger King—had pretty much locked up the nationwide fast food hamburger market by then while regionals like Jack In The Box, Carl's Jr, and Hardees continued to thrive. At one time Burger Chef was second only to McDonald's in number of locations. They had a fantastic dry but tasty Roast Beef sandwich that Hardees continued to sell for years alongside a most excellent fried chicken which I assume was dropped because it couldn't be prepared properly by a minimum wage worker. Schroeder's Drive-In in Danville, Illinois was last to serve the original Burger Chef menu items, they closed in 2015. Fans in Jacksonville, Illinois can hop over to CR's Drive-In where they still make Burger Chef french fries.

Krystal

Speaking of regionals, Krystal was the first fast food chain in the South whereas White Castle (the oldest hamburger franchise in the United States) was more of a northern, midwest, and west coast thing. The Krystal burger was a straight up ripoff of White Castle's, if you liked one you'd probably enjoy the other. More than a decade ago Krystal stores were upgraded, reviving a slumbering giant that first awoke back in 1932.

Celebrity Fried Chicken

Where were you during the Fried Chicken Wars of the early-1970s? After Kentucky Fried Chicken's incredible success Roy Rogers, Mahalia Jackson, Minnie Pearl, Tex Ritter, Tennessee Ernie Ford, and even Popeye began slinging drumsticks and thighs. They (mostly) quietly faded away, not lasting long enough to spread too far from their point of origin. Popeye's continues to flourish on a worldwide scale, what the heck did Popeye ever have to do with chicken, fried or otherwise? I'm dying to know how Mahalia Jackson's "Glori-fried" chicken tasted but the last outlet in Nashville closed a few years ago.

Roy Rogers Family Restaurant

I miss Roy Rogers' fare, very popular in the 1970s. The secret to their sandwich was *it was made with actual roast beef* that they cooked in-store, served on a lightly toasted sesame seed bun. Today's roast beef standard, Arby's, slices off of a molded gelatinous meat concoction that doesn't fit my definition of real beef. In 2005, I was traveling to New York City quite a bit to do TV and discovered the New Jersey landscape dotted with Roy Rogers restaurants beckoning from rest stops along the highways. I couldn't resist sampling their Roast Beef again, a faint echo of the terrific sandwich they used to serve. My life has been in pursuit of fine tasting Roast Beef sandwiches and I will continue my journey—but doubt if any fast food item will ever again satisfy that craving.

Who Killed TV's
Superman?

Starring

GEORGE REEVES

Almost every kid who grew up in the '60s heard a story of how George Reeves died. Depending on which version you heard, TV's Superman, thinking he was the character he portrayed (or despondent over being typecast), jumped off a building to see if he really could fly (or put a gun to his head and shot himself).

The coroner's report officially ruled the death a suicide, stating that the star was killed by a single gunshot to the head in the early morning hours of June 16, 1959. Truth is, we may never know the whole story; intrigue and confusion cloud the issue to this day. Many people who have taken a hard look at the case agree that murder, not suicide, was a much more likely scenario.

George Reeves was a moderately successful film actor in 1951 when he accepted the role of Superman in the feature film Superman and the Mole Men. A television series underwritten by Kellogg's for first-run syndication was put into production with the same cast just a few days after filming on the feature concluded.

When The Adventures of Superman debuted in late 1952, it was a big hit, by far the most imaginative and exciting adventure series the medium had ever seen. Even though there were no color televisions available to the public, in 1954 The Adventures of Superman became only the second TV series to be filmed in color (Cisco Kid was the first). This was a prescient move undertaken to make the show more commercially viable in the future.

When the series ceased production after six successful seasons, George Reeves found himself typecast as the Man of Steel and good roles became scarce. Despite a couple of lean years, things began to turn around in 1959.

The producers of The Adventures of Superman decided to film another season's worth of shows in 1960 and Reeves agreed to return, signing on with a hefty raise. He was scheduled to shoot a film in Spain, and was to be married to his fiancée Lenore Lemmon on June 19, 1959—just three days after his supposed suicide.

There was another side to George Reeves that went unreported in the press—this was a guy who liked to party. Late night booze fests were common at his home on Benedict Canyon. Reeves enjoyed the LA nightlife as well, and ran into some shady characters along the way. He engaged in a seven-year affair with Toni Mannix, the wife of Eddie Mannix, an extremely well-known, powerful MGM executive with

reported mob ties. Mannix was in poor health and aware of their relationship. People who knew the couple assumed that George and Toni would marry after Eddie was no longer around.

Toni Mannix was devastated when their relationship came to a halt in 1958. Reeves' new love, Lenore Lemmon, stated that the jilted lover was calling Reeves repeatedly at all hours of the day and night, harassing the actor for months before his death. So much so that Reeves retained an attorney to try to convince the disturbed woman to stop the calls that were coming up to twenty times a day, calls that were sometimes nothing more than annoying hang-ups. The attorney wasn't persuasive, according to Lemmon, and the harassment continued unabated.

On the night of June 15, 1959, Lemmon, Reeves, and two guests were partying at the actor's home. At about 1:15 the next morning, George Reeves went upstairs to bed. He had been drinking heavily and was under the influence of painkillers prescribed for injuries he sustained in a car accident.

Moments later, a shot rang out upstairs. The actor was found dead, sprawled out on his bed, naked, with a bullet hole in his right temple. When police arrived, the death was treated as a suicide since all of the houseguests agreed there could be no other explanation. There was no sign of forced entry and the high alcohol content in the actor's blood, in combination with narcotics, made suicide a strong possibility.

Was there another explanation? Police at the scene wondered about two fresh bullet holes found in the bedroom walls. Lenore Lemmon explained that she had accidentally fired the gun earlier when she was fooling around with it.

There were no powder marks from the gun's discharge on the actor's wound so the weapon would have to have been held several inches from the head before firing, most unusual in a suicide. There were reportedly no fingerprints on the pistol and the actor's hands were not tested for gunpowder residue.

Many who knew Reeves at the time agreed that the actor was happier than

he had been in years, looking forward to his upcoming marriage, and eager to begin another season of his still-popular television series. Money wasn't a issue either—he wasn't super-rich, but the actor was still being paid residuals every time Superman was rerun in major markets.

Still in mourning over her fiancée's death, Lenore Lemmon suffered another indignity when the will was read—Reeves' entire estate was left to Toni Mannix, who said the actor must have meant the money and the house on Benedict Canyon to help the charities that they both worked with. "Toni got a house for charity and I got a broken heart," was Lemmon's dramatic statement to the press.

Leading the charge for more concrete answers about what transpired that fateful night was George Reeves' mother, who held up cremation of the body for three years while noted Hollywood investigator Jerry Geisler looked into unanswered questions surrounding the highly suspicious death. Both Geisler and Reeves' mother died of natural causes before they could prove foul play was involved.

Had someone entered the house, a person with a gun and a ruthless reputation, murdered the television star and warned everyone in the home to stay silent about what happened? Superman producer Tommy Carr thought so, and said so for years in interviews. Co-stars Noel Neill (Lois Lane) and Jack Larson (Jimmy Olsen) generated publicity

for the case in the late '80s, maintaining in press and TV interviews that foul play was indeed the cause of death. After thirty years, they were trying to keep the case alive by asking for a more thorough inquiry into the troubling circumstances surrounding the "suicide" of their old friend.

Oddly, in a 1998 edition of USA Today, Larson reversed himself and stated emphatically that he believed Reeves did commit suicide and that Larson's longtime friend Toni Mannix (recently deceased) definitely had nothing to do with it. He didn't want her memory sullied by unfounded accusations.

Another theory has it that Reeves and Lemmon argued that night and Lemmon shot her lover in the heat of the moment. But why would her guests—witnesses to a crime—risk their reputations and freedom to cover for her? Perhaps someone will provide new clues to this puzzling mystery but with the passage of time, that becomes more and more unlikely.

Because the facts here are so murky, I asked George Reeves expert Jim Nolt what his thoughts on the case were. Jim was an on-camera consultant when the television show Unsolved Mysteries did a segment on this baffling story.

Here are his comments:

"Almost from the moment the fatal shot was fired, friends of George Reeves have been questioning what happened in the early morning hours of June 16, 1959. Lenore Lemmon said George killed himself because he could find no work after Superman, but many who knew George remain skeptical to this day. No one is even sure who was in the house that night, and we have only Lenore Lemmon's word for the happenings. According to Lemmon, the only people in the house that night, in addition to George and herself, were Carol Von Ronkle, William Bliss, and writer Robert Condon.

"Lemmon says George Reeves committed suicide. However, no fingerprints were found on the gun, no powder burns were on George's head wound. No powder burns were found on his hands. The spent shell was found underneath his body . . . the gun on the floor between his feet . . . the bullet in the ceiling. Other bullet holes were found in the bedroom floor, and the bullets were recovered from the living room below. Were all the shots fired at the same time, or were the other bullets fired days . . . perhaps weeks earlier?

"We do know Lenore Lemmon and the other guests had been drinking. Indeed, Reeves' blood alcohol level was .27, well above the point of being intoxicated. The police were not called for thirty to forty-five minutes after Reeves' death, but Lemmon never explained why she waited so long to notify the authorities.

There is no doubt Lenore Lemmon and George Reeves had a volatile relationship. They were seen arguing in public earlier in the evening. Could that argument have continued back at 1579 Benedict Canyon Drive? I believe it's quite likely and that George's death was the result of that argument. If Lenore did shoot George, it would have simply been easier for her to say it was suicide. It would save much time and energy on her part explaining how it all happened. None of the other guests ever gave public testimony regarding the events of that night, and Lenore left California the next day never to return."

We also heard from expert Michael J. Hayde on the subject, an on-camera consultant for the Unsolved Mysteries segment on Reeves' death.

"There is so much more to the story than can be told here, and even the book Hollywood Kryptonite didn't do as thorough a job as it should have (spending more time on a sensationalized and exaggerated account of Reeves' night life and attitude toward Superman).

"Even to say that the police botched the investigation is simplistic. The day after the autopsy, when Chief Parker announced that he 'was satisfied with the verdict' of suicide, there were two LAPD detectives in Reeves' bedroom pulling up a carpet to discover the other bullet holes. Why, if the case had just been closed? By then, Lemmon had left town for good, and there was no evidence to link Eddie Mannix or his wife to the crime. Without witnesses or a credible confession, there was just an overwhelming amount of circumstantial evidence, which implicated no one."

I can't help but think about the final two lines of dialogue from the last episode of The Adventures of Superman broadcast in 1958. Jimmy Olsen fawns, "Golly, Mr. Kent, you'll never know how wonderful it is to be like Superman." George Reeves (as Clark Kent) replies, "No, Jimmy, I guess I never will," giving a wink to the camera, a sly goodbye to us all, before fading into electronic oblivion.

Excerpt from TVparty! Television's Untold Tales

THE END

AMOS 'N' ANDY

Standard & Stain

When the CBS and NBC networks presented their 75th Anniversary extravaganzas in the early 2000s there was an historically important milestone turned millstone that was ignored. In the thirties and forties life in America came to a virtual standstill when Amos 'n' Andy was on the air. Movie theaters would stop the feature so folks could listen to two white guys pretending to be three black guys.

THE BEGINNING

In 1917, Sidney Smith created the popular newspaper comic strip The Gumps, depicting lower middle class family life. Freeman Gosden and Charles Correll were slated to play The Gumps for a proposed radio program in

1926. Before the show made it on the air the two actors decided instead to create their own variation on the theme, a radio series with comic strip style continuity. On January 12, 1926, Sam n' Henry became radio's first original serial and the first to feature continuing characters and storylines from week to week.

Broadcast over WGN, Sam 'n' Henry was the story of two simple-minded rural guys trying to make it in the big city of Chicago. Although never specifically identified as black it was certainly understood, Correll and Gosden voiced the characters with the kind of exaggerated Negro dialect familiar in minstrel shows of the day. Gosden confessed to a reporter in 1981, "We chose black characters because blackface comics could tell funnier stories than whiteface comics."

In their five day a week, fifteen-minute program, Gosden and Correll became the first entertainers to master the intimacy that radio promised and, in the process, invented the basic model for every radio and television program that followed.

Sam and Henry were roughhewn caricatures, reflecting the prevailing racial prejudices of the era, frequently drunk and occasionally in trouble with the law (they were arrested for gambling in an early episode).

The program was so popular Correll and Gosden performed regularly on stage in blackface for which they earned $2000 a week, a staggering amount in 1927. There were several brisk-selling Victor 78 RPM records by Sam 'n' Henry, routines recorded especially for vinyl.

However successful their outside ventures Correll and Gosden (writing all the scripts and playing all the major roles) were making only $100 a week for the radio broadcast itself. With Chicago ratings through the roof they reasoned Sam 'n Henry would go over just as big with a national audience. WGN disagreed.

The production moved to WMAQ, another Chicago station that believed in its potential. Amos 'n' Andy (renamed because WGN owned the name Sam n' Henry) began in March, 1928 over WMAQ and thirty-eight affiliates stretching from the East Coast to San Francisco. By distributing the series in this fashion Correll and Gosden created the syndication marketplace. A year after its debut Amos 'n' Andy had become a nationwide phenomenon.

NETWORK

Amos 'n' Andy was broadcast nationally over the NBC radio network beginning in August of 1929, sponsored by Pepsodent. The laconic opening tune, The Perfect Song, was one of the classic themes of radio's golden age, a lilting ditty reminiscent of the (supposed) lazy days of the Old South.

Successful from the start the show's popularity rested on the novelty of listening in on two negroes attempting to relate to the sophisticated world of tele-phones and motor cars. Still written entirely by the two white stars, Amos 'n' Andy was the top-rated program of all in 1930, with a 54.4 ratings share and 30 million listeners (compare that to the 2014 Super Bowl's 70 share, the most watched telecast of all time) due to the wily, coniving George 'Kingfish' Stevens supplanting sensible Amos as star of the show (Freeman Gosden gave voice to both Amos and Kingfish; Charles Correll played Andrew H. Brown).

Critic Arthur H. Samuels opined in the New Yorker, "With half a dozen plots running through their sketches, they hold the dramatic tension in a way to arouse the admiration of Professor Baker. For a week, the Kingfish's Great Home Bank tottered on the brink of ruin and thousands of families all over America never ate a dinner in peace. The night that the Great Home Bank toppled over, with Madam Queen's fifty dollars involved in the ruin,

MINUTE INTERVIEWS WITH STARS OF THE AIR ON KSD

IN THE BEGINNING THEY USED NO FEMININE CHARACTERS IN THEIR SKETCHES, BUT LATER AFTER THEY HAD MARRIED, FEMALE IMPERSONATIONS CAME INTO EVIDENCE.

INCIDENTLY, THE PARTNERS HAVE BEEN PALS SINCE 1919 WHEN THEY BOTH WORKED AS BACK STAGE EMPLOYEES IN A SMALL-TIME SHOW.

AMOS 'N' ANDY

FREEMAN F. GOSDEN   CHARLES J. CORRELL

WITHOUT DOUBT THEIR SOUTHERN HOME-LIFE HAS BEEN IMMEASURABLY HELPFUL IN MAKING THEIR FAMOUS RADIO SKIT SO CLOSELY ADHERE TO TRUE NEGRO CHARACTERIZATIONS.

was the blackest since that night in October after the stock market dive."

Listening with a modern ear it's hard to get through more than five minutes of early Amos 'n' Andy. Hardly anything ever happened, just mundane boring daily conversations. One episode opened with a three-minute, one-sided phone call consisting of Andy talking a female into keeping a date with the Kingfish.

That same year a book was published, All About Amos 'n' Andy and Their Creators Correll & Gosden, and a major motion picture released entitled Check and Double Check. The film, with Correll and Gosden in blackface, was a dreadful abomination on several levels not the least of which—it was boring.

Regardless, Check and Double Check was one of the highest grossing films of 1930 so Correll and Gosden once again corked their faces in Paramount's The Big Broadcast of 1936. There would be no more film roles for the duo.

There was a series of Amos 'n' Andy cartoons from Official Films with the original radio voices and insulting character designs that looked like they were drawn by MAD comic artist Basil Wolverton. The depiction of African-Americans in these shorts was one of bug-eyed, white-lipped darkies—objects d'ridicule.

CONTROVERSY BEGINS

The Pittsburgh Courier, the second-largest Black-owned newspaper in the country in the 1930s, fanned the flames of a growing grassroots

controversy in order to get radio's most popular show thrown off the air. It was part community activism, part circulation ploy considering the prevailing culture.

"Our protest has the sanction of all intelligent people, white and black," a Courier editorial read in 1931. "We do not expect ignorant Negroes and whites to be able to see the insult. We are not looking for the Amos 'n' Andy Negro to join our protest. We are happy to have the intelligence of both races endorsing our program. It has grown beyond the proportions of a joke; it has reached the serious stage. We are going on--with the help of all, if possible, but without the help of the ignorant, if we must."

By the mid-thirties, there were Amos 'n' Andy imitations like Honeyboy and Sassafras (recording artists George Fields and Johnnie Welsh) and Molasses and January starring Pick Malone and Pat Padgett, heard on the Maxwell House Show Boat from 1932 through 1937. These 'Negro' roles were played by whites as well.

By contrast, there were almost no real black voices on the radio. Among the few were Tess Gardella as Aunt Jemima airing 1931-33 and Ernest Whitman and Eddie Green (billed as "network radio's only colored comedians") in The Gibson Family from 1934-35. Eddie "Rochester" Anderson joined The Jack Benny Show in 1937 and Paducah Plantation starring Clarence Muse could be heard from 1936-37.

Though they openly complained about pressure from civil rights groups, NBC banned the word 'nigger' from the airwaves in 1935. That ban held until Sanford and Son debuted in 1972.

For the first seven years of Amos 'n' Andy's run there were no actresses, women were talked about by the guys. In 1939, the first regular African-American cast member was added, Ernestine Wade. Initially cast as Andy's date she inherited the role of Sapphire Stevens, the Kingfish's long-suffering wife—also known as 'the Battle-Ax.'

A Christmas tradition began in 1940 when Amos explained the meaning of Lord's Prayer at his daughter Arbadella's bedside. This script was repeated every Christmas season through 1954, varying only slightly from year to year.

Freeman F. Gosden, Jr., son of one of the creators, recalled those Christmas shows. "It is probably safe to conclude that more people heard Amos' description of the Lord's Prayer than that of anyone else in the world. There is no question that he felt this was his proudest lifetime achievement. We would go to the studio and watch the show from the client's booth. Then Dad would bring the recording home and after dinner play it over and over again until midnight, with tears in his eyes."

An Amos 'n' Andy 78 RPM record with 'The Lord's Prayer' on one side and 'Little Bitty Baby' on the other was released, backed by the Jeff Alexander Choir in addition to an Amos 'n' Andy box set with four records of past radio shows.

Though still a top series ratings had been slowly declining for a decade; for the 1942-43 season Amos 'n' Andy scored a dismal 9.4. By 1943, partly due to wartime product shortages, sponsor Campbell's Soup announced they could no longer afford the budget so the series was being dropped. On February 19, 1943, Andrew H. Brown and the Kingfish uncharacteristically took full-time jobs in a defense plant. The Amos 'n' Andy saga came to an end. For the time being.

REINVENTION

After 4,091 episodes as a fifteen-minute, daily comedy-drama, Amos 'n' Andy returned to the airwaves as a weekly 30-minute sitcom on Friday, October 8, 1943, sponsored by Rinso. What the 1943 version of the show had going for it was a thrilling opening that made listeners believe big-time entertainment was on its way. And, comparatively, it was.

Correll and Gosden considered casting black actors in the lead roles for the new format and recorded several auditions before ultimately deciding to return to the roles they made famous, supported by an expanded African-American cast. Joining regulars Ernestine Wade and Elinor Harriot during the 1943-44 season were Ruby Dandridge, Ernest Whitman, Lillian Randolph, James Baskett, and Jester Hairston.

Over the years black actors Amanda Randolph (Lillian's sister), Roy Glenn, Johnny Lee (as lawyer Algonquin J. Calhoun), Milly Bruce, Amos Reese and others joined the cast. White voice artists like Jean Van Der Pyle (Wilma Flintstone) and Mel Blanc (who voiced hundreds of cartoon characters) could be heard in later years.

Special guest stars stepped up to the microphone every week including Ginger Rogers, Edward G. Robinson, Walter Huston, Peter Lorre, Lionel Barrymore and other major celebrities. That angle was dropped in February, 1944 but not before legendary actress / blues singer Ethel Waters did a turn playing herself as a glamorous celebrity.

Scriptwriters were brought on board for the first time and the show was performed before a live audience. Ratings nearly doubled for the new half-hour series, garnering an respectable 17.1 for the 1943-44 season. Gary Williams wrote to the TVparty! web site: "I am an African-American (35 years old) and a big fan of Amos 'n' Andy, especially the radio series. The TV series was also funny. When Gosden and Correll started the program in 1928, they based the show on people they knew. Both men were from the South and they were surrounded by black people. "If you take an unbiased look at the characters, the majority of them held respectable jobs and owned their own businesses. The only exceptions were Andy and the Kingfish. Even Lightnin', as dense as he was, was a janitor and there is nothing wrong with that. But you had lawyer Calhoun, Shorty the barber, and of course Amos, owner of the Fresh Air Taxicab Company.

"A lot of the shows today, and even in the '70's, made a big deal about people's color. If you take a look at the Amos 'n' Andy scripts from both radio and television there are not too many instances where the characters mention they are black, nor do they complain that the 'white man has everything and we don't because we're black.' These were average people, who just happened to be black.

"I once attended a class on cultural diversity where I brought in a copy of an Amos 'n' Andy radio series and a Lum and Abner radio show (Lum and Abner were two backwoods hillbilly characters created by Chester Lauck and Norris Goff around the same time as Amos 'n' Andy.) I played them both and, although both shows have stereotypes that can be considered negative, no one wanted to talk about Lum and Abner, they just wanted to talk about Amos 'n' Andy. The plots of Amos 'n' Andy could fit into many other situation comedies. In fact, I read where a number of Amos 'n' Andy scripts were reused and turned up in... Leave It To Beaver! This was because Joe Connelly and Bob Mosher wrote both shows."

In 1946, Amos 'n' Andy joined NBC's 'Must Hear' Tuesday night lineup of Fibber McGee and Molly, Bob Hope, and Red Skelton. Ratings soared. Bright musical numbers performed by a full orchestra punctuated the scripts with tunes vocalized by The Jubilaires and, alternately in 1947, the Delta Rhythm Boys.

Routines performed by the Rhythm Boys included swinging versions of popular songs like Route 66, a comical tune about Lightnin,' and a salute to the controversial Disney film Song of the South. The Jubilaires were more spiritual in nature with Joshua Fit The Battle of Jerico and an ode to the Emancipation Proclamation that contained the lyrics, "You can take a boat or you can take a train. That's how it's always been and how it will remain. As long as all of us keep ridin,' keep ridin,' keep ridin' on the freedom train."

Often these musical interludes veered too close to the lingering image of 'happy darkies singing by the riverside.' But then the network wasn't particularly worried about offending anyone— advertisers weren't anxious to reach a black audience. Only about one in fifteen African-American homes had a radio in 1946. Outside of the larger cities, there was no measurable economic pull in the black community. With ratings continuing to rise over the decade, reaching a 23 share by 1948, it was time to expand the franchise.

Blatz presents... **Amos 'n'**

The Amos 'n' Andy radio program switched nights—and network—on October 10, 1948 when Correll and Gosden sold all rights to the series to CBS for something close to $2.5 million. The Paley Raid as it was known (William Paley was the head of CBS), netted CBS many of NBC's highest rated stars including Jack Benny and Red Skelton.

Amos 'n' Andy could now be heard on Sunday nights at 7:30pm still

Andy on TV!

sponsored by Rinso, "with Solium, the sunlight ingredient." As a major component of the network family Amos 'n' Andy was instrumental in selling lots of CBS brand TVs and radio receivers in the early-fifties

In the toddler days of television, priority number one for the networks was transitioning their most recognized franchises from radio to the new medium. This was especially true of radio's biggest, longest-running hit

Amos 'n' Andy. Correll and Gosden toyed with different concepts, including shooting the TV show with African-American actors and overdubbing their voices. At CBS's request, Fred De Cordova (future Tonight Show with Johnny Carson producer) filmed the first TV pilot with Correll and Gosden playing themselves as white men in addition to their roles as Kingfish, Amos and Andy in blackface. "They were heavy stockholders in CBS and decided they were interested in appearing as themselves and as Amos and Andy in a television series," De Cordova stated years later. "I was selected to direct. it was stressed that the project was to be kept under wraps, no publicity at all."

After filming the half-hour pilot with guest stars James Mason, Geoffery Holder and Diahann Carroll, everyone was pleased with the results but decided not to go forward. Fred De Cordova explained, "I was instructed to take the tape—the sole evidence of the project—proceed to the incinerator and make sure that every bit of it burned up."

An extensive nationwide talent search was launched to cast the principal roles with black actors, a painstaking process that lasted nearly three years with hundreds of individual auditions.

Esteemed stage actor Alvin Childress was cast as sensible cab driver Amos (still relegated to minor character status despite first billing in the show's title), "race movie" director/star Spencer Williams Jr. as gullible Andy and retired vaudeville legend Tim Moore as the Kingfish. The familiar African-American performers already lending their voices to the radio series were brought over to the TV version—including Ernestine Wade, Amanda Randolph, Johnnie Lee, Jester Hairston, and Roy Glenn.

Horace Stewart was seen as Lightnin', a lazy, slow-talking Stephen Fetchit-type janitor—the most racially insensitive character. The vaudevillian (known alternately as Nick Stewart and Nick O'Demus) was originally offered the role of lawyer Algonquin J. Calhoun on the TV version but turned it down, unwilling to play a blatantly stereotypical role. When another call came to audition for the part of Lightnin' he reconsidered. The money would help him realize his lifelong dream of starting a theater where black actors could excel in parts other than maids and butlers.

Shot at the Hal Roach Studios in February of 1951, Amos 'n' Andy was the first CBS program to be filmed on the West Coast. Based on a 1949 radio script by Mosher and Connell, the pilot episode was directed by Abby Berlin (the Blondie movie series). Famed Universal comedy director Charles

Barton (Abbott and Costello films) took over as director on the series after that.

TV's Amos 'n' Andy had all of the elements of an enduring classic—first-rate scripts that would rival the best episode of I Love Lucy or Seinfeld for hilarious plot weavings along with lovable characters played with aplomb by masterful actors clearly in their element. But there was an inescapable component to Amos 'n' Andy that overshadowed the superior accomplishments of the performers and production staff—the principals were black and the year was 1951.

Like most fifties' sitcoms, Amos 'n' Andy contained broad, comic characterizations and outlandish plotlines. The stories had nothing to do with race, and on a positive note, introduced the concept of dignified black doctors, business leaders, cops and lawyers—a first for any mass medium.

Here's a typical exchange between Saffire and the Kingfish from the TV show:

Saffire: "Here's the address, George. Mr. Baxter is holding the job open for you at the construction company. Now you go down there and get it."

Kingfish: "Yeah, but honey. Shovelin' sand into a cement mixer, that ain't my line of work. You see, I'm more the executive, Dictaphone, button-pushin' type."

Saffire: "You go down there and see Mr. Baxter and get that job. He's only holding it for you because he's an old friend of my family's."

Kingfish: "Honey, I

can't just go bustin' in there and start throwin' sand around. I got to have references and it'll probably take me two or three weeks to get somebody to referend a good word for me."

Saffire: "You get over here and go. I've already told Mr. Baxter all about you."

Kingfish: "And he's still willin' to hire me, huh?"

Saffire: "Don't look so glum, George. You'll like your job after you get started."

Kingfish: "That's what I afraid of, Honey. I afraid I get to like the job so well and stay there year after year and never leave. First thing you know, I in a rut. And that ain't good for me."

Saffire: "George, you won't be there long. You'll move on to a better job."

Kingfish: "Well, then it seems silly to get settled in dis one and then have to leave right away again. Why not wait 'till a better job show up?"

When Kingfish finally shows up for work, it goes like this:

Mr. Baxter (boss): "Now this will be your job, Stevens. You shovel sand from this pile into the cement mixer."

Kingfish: "Oh, dat's fine, Mr. Baxter. I'll go shop around for a shovel. I remember a pretty good shovel store up in Connecticut."

Mr. Baxter: "You don't have to buy a shovel, we give you one. Now how about getting to work?"

Kingfish: "Is this an all day job?"

Mr. Baxter: "You'll put in a full day. Eight to five, you'll work."

Kingfish: "Eight to five... what's the odds if I don't work?"

Mr. Baxter: "Look Stevens, your wife told me you'd try to weasel your way out of this job but she gave me strict instructions not to let you. Are you going to start now or in the morning?"

Kingfish: "Well... it's nine o clock now and you quit at five. The day pretty well shot. I'll see you in the morning."

Protests over the TV series began immediately. Times being what they were it was inappropriate, no matter how excellent the writing, to portray blacks as buffoons if there were no other programs on television featuring African-Americans in more serious roles. And there weren't. There was no balance. Civil rights leaders and the NAACP targeted Amos 'n' Andy as a twenty-five year ongoing insult that had to be stopped before it spread even further.

Ratings were strong for the first season, the thirteenth most popular show of the season. But because of the growing controversy, and with ratings falling during year two, sponsor Blatz Beer dropped the production after season two. CBS filmed another thirteen episodes (that were never aired during primetime) to make a more attractive syndication package.

TV BLACKOUT

The network found itself in a bind, receiving hate mail from the South when blacks were shown interacting positively with whites, and weathering protests from blacks when they were depicted as ignorant and deferential. With racial tension growing around the nation skittish advertisers didn't want to appear pro-black by sponsoring a show starring African-Americans.

To avoid future headaches, TV producers and the networks largely avoided casting persons of color altogether from 1953 until 1968. You could count on one hand the number of African-Americans that played significant continuing roles on a TV series during that fifteen year period. CBS president William Paley wrote in his book As It Happened, "Gosden and Correll had created a warm and funny fantasy world in the listener's imagination on radio. When that world became visual, it also became concrete and literal. Amos 'n' Andy remained on radio in some form until 1960. But the television series, under attack by black leaders for its entire life, left the network after two seasons."

TVparty-er Charles L. tells of us of his experience watching the show in the fifties, "I am an African-American. I loved the Amos 'n' Andy show and grieved when it was discontinued. I think people failed to realize that comedy has an element of ridicule - that is why it is funny.

"As a small child in the fifties I didn't care about stereotypes and the like. All I knew was there were Blacks on television. I, and my parents, lived for the Amos 'n' Andy show. We would laugh and enjoy ourselves while it was on. It really hurt us when the show was taken off the air. What an injustice. There were no longer any blacks on television that we could take pride in, only the occasional guest appearance of Mahalia Jackson or Pearl Bailey on the Ed Sullivan show. If the show had been allowed to continue, I don't think we would have had to wait until the 1980's for a Cosby Show. How many black actors were denied a chance because black shows were seen as too risky or controversial? Sometimes, in our diligence to make things better, we actually shoot ourselves in the foot."

After the TV series was dropped from prime time in 1953 CBS began syndicating Amos 'n' Andy reruns to local stations where it attracted consistently strong numbers, especially in rural areas and down South—the first hit syndicated television show.

Another viewer Chris Wood experienced it this way, "I am a child of the economically segregated suburbs of New York City. When I was growing up in the 1950s, I watched the reruns of Amos 'n' Andy. I thought nothing about these people being foolish black stereotypes.

"In fact, quite the contrary. Most of the news coming from New York City only showed blacks in the worst light—criminals or in dire poverty. It was not until I went to college that I realized there was a black middle class. I always thought they existed only in the South since the New York news showed only poverty.

"Anyway, if we put aside color and look at the characters, for every negative attribute there was a corresponding white male who was portrayed the same.

"Amos, owner of his own business—Herbert T. Gillis on Dobie Gillis

"Andy, an unemployed male—Lou Costello on Abbott and Costello and Freddie on My Little Margie.

"Kingfish, the crafty con man—Ralph Kramden on The Honeymooners and Eddie Haskell on Leave it to Beaver.

"Lighting, the dumb/slow/fool—Lumpy on Leave it to Beaver and Gilligan on Gilligan's Island.

"A.J. Calhoun, shyster lawyer—Angel (comic relief) on the Rockford Files (and a felon to boot!).

"And could you get much more foolish and condescending than the Beverly Hillbillies and their horrendous spin-offs?

"These characters were (are) funny because of characterizations, not white, black or otherwise. In fact, the comedy shows thereafter that tried to show 'race' in a positive light don't hold up over time (Chico and the Man, even Sanford and Son).

"Amos 'n' Andy was a chance to see real middle class blacks in a cross section of a working class neighborhood. My parents were both born and raised in Manhattan, in fact my father was from what is now known as Spanish Harlem. He reminded us that, although we rarely came in contact with people of color in lily-white suburbia, his life in a working class section of Irish, Hispanic, Italian and African-Americans was lived pretty much in the same way as the Harlem of Amos 'n' Andy - because they were all in the same economic situation.

"Still, I can understand the feelings of blacks at the time. But what passes for comedy now makes one yearn for the scripts of Amos 'n' Andy."

Bill Cosby expressed the opposite view in an interview with Playboy magazine in 1969, "That show still gets to me, man. Each time I name an Amos 'n' Andy character, try to imagine these guys as white, and you won't be able to: You had Lightnin', who was slow in every way; Calhoun, the lawyer who never got anyone out of trouble and never went into court prepared; Kingfish the conniver, who was always saying, 'Yeah, but Brother Andy...' and Andy himself, who wasn't too bright either. Like, nobody on that show was bright except Amos, the cabdriver, who we hardly ever heard from. And then there was the Kingfish's wife Saffire. Every time she came through that door she'd be chewing him out for something. Now, audiences weren't supposed to laugh with these people they were supposed to laugh at them because they were so dumb."

Esteemed writer James Oliver Killens was more harsh in his assessment, "I accuse Hollywood of being the most anti-Negro influence in this nation... it created the lying, stealing, childish, eyeball-rolling, foot-shuffling, sex-obsessed, teeth-showing, dice-shooting black male, and told the world this was the real negro in the USA."

ANOTHER FORMAT CHANGE

Though they were never seen in the video version, Freeman F. Gosden and Charles J. Correll continued voicing Kingfish, Amos and Andy on the radio program while sharing the same supporting cast as the TV production.

An intense controversy over the television program erupted in June, 1951 while the radio show was on hiatus. This resulted in an unexpected ratings upswing when the radio program returned in October, 1951. Amos 'n' Andy kicked off the fifties attracting an audience of more than 30 million listeners, #1 again.

After nearly a decade of surging audience numbers there was an alarming drop of ten million listeners during the 1953-54 season (down a total of twenty million from their peak in 1948). But it was radio itself that was on the wane, television had become the chosen medium for home entertainment. Longtime radio sitcoms like Fibber McGee and Molly and The Great Gildersleeve were falling by the wayside at an rapid rate. Their stalwart hits almost all flopped on TV.

The CBS radio program Amos 'n' Andy was cancelled in 1954, replaced by—Amos 'n' Andy.

The Amos 'n' Andy Music Hall, a half-hour, nightly recorded music show bracketed by comedy bits began in the fall of 1954, replacing the sonic sitcom. Apart from longtime announcer Harlow Wilcox there was only Gosden & Correll in front of the microphone playing their three familiar roles accompanied by canned laughter and applause. Early episodes featured guest stars like Jack Benny and Liberace.

In this new format George 'Kingfish' Stevens was front and center as master of ceremonies of the Lodge Hall radio station, helped along by pals Amos and Andy. Sponsored by Kool cigarettes, this program most closely resembled the earliest Amos 'n' Andy broadcasts with Joe Connelly and Bob Mosher writing the comedy bits and no supporting players.

The Amos 'n' Andy Music Hall would open with a thin plotline that meandered along four or five minutes at a time, wrapping around pop music hits by artists like Ella Fitzgerald, Ray Anthony, Perry Como, Bobby Darin, and Dean Martin. Only seven million listeners stuck around for the Music Hall incarnation. Without the high costs associated with a network series it was still a profitable venture for CBS.

This program ran into protests as well. African-American soldiers complained when this show was carried over the Armed Forces network and they were forced to listen to it. They demanded it's removal and prevailed.

The Amos 'n' Andy Music Hall ran until November 25, 1960. The curtain had finally rung for old-time radio programs, the type Amos 'n' Andy gave birth to. In 1966, a time when only 1% of African-American men were working in professional positions, civil rights leaders finally convinced CBS to withdraw the Amos 'n' Andy TV series from syndication. TVparty-er Deverett tells us, "I am a black female, born and still living in the South. I watched Amos 'n' Andy reruns and actually raced home to see them. Can you imagine, a young black girl in the south able to watch black people on TV? It was encouraging, not discouraging.

"I knew that blacks were not buffoons, shiftless and lazy. I lived in a house and a community where black people were hardworking, educated and law abiding. Even as a child, I knew the pranks on Amos 'n' Andy were just that, pranks on a TV show—for entertainment. I applaud the NAACP for their efforts in working to remove racial stigmas. However, I wish this generation could see some of those shows. I have some on video cassette and at first my children didn't want to watch. Not because of the content but because it wasn't in color! We would laugh at Calhoun, Andy, Kingfish, Sapphire and her mother.

"I know the actors received criticism for working on such a show, even then. But I found it, and still find it, entertaining. Looking at it from the standpoint of being degrading to blacks, I find it no more insulting than Sanford and Son—or as embarrassing as All In The Family should have been to whites."

The Torture and Savage Slaying
of the East Coast Rave King

LeBrun

Ed LeBrun was the heart and soul of Greensboro's surging supersonic rave scene two decades ago. When Babylon opened downtown in 1994 LeBrun's frenzied First Friday parties brought down the House, booking world renowned DJs—Diesel Boy, Andy Hughes, Bad Boy Bill, Frankie Bones, Ani (On-E), Bobble, Derrick Carter, Keoki, Sven Väth—who held thousands of hyperactive, jumped-up, sweaty club kids from as far away as Florida and New York in a thrall.

The owner of Spins Compact Discs & Tapes in the Lawndale shopping center LeBrun was an essential conduit for ravers around the world, thanked on dozens of seminal dance music releases. Chris Kennedy worked at Spins, "It was the go-to spot for upcoming rave flyers, mix tapes, rare vinyl, and many other things that reflected our culture. If Ed knew you and you asked real nice and bought the blanks from him, he would make you bootleg tapes of all the parties. Mix CDs that were legal and released under a label were rare, simply because many of the records used samples that were unlicensed. This made the culture feel different and unique because having tunes to listen to outside of the party was next to impossible unless you went to Spins.

"He sold the legit Technics 1200s and did a great deal of special ordering for a lot of the DJs, music that was next to impossible to come by any other way than knowing someone who had access to the many different independent record companies, most of them overseas."

Soft spoken with a shy smile, LeBrun began promoting electronic music nights in the late 1980s at Kilroys before expanding into larger, more exotic locales that only a select few were privy to. "We had to meet someone in the UNCG parking lot on Aycock in order to get a flyer with the directions." That's how Chris Kennedy rolled, "You only really saw most of these people at parties because we all came from different walks of life and from different areas in and around the state. It was like leading a second, secret life that you really cared a lot more about than work or school. It really was it's own culture and Ed was pretty close to being the center of it for most of us.

"Ed managed to rent the Depot in downtown Greensboro on a few occasions. No one seemed to care much about the Depot at that time, since it wasn't actively being used. What blew our minds the first time we saw it was the lighted dance floor. We didn't know anything about the disco years other than what we heard from our parents but it seemed to us like we had found a forgotten discotheque and brought it through time with us into the future. It was amazing, one of my all time favorite party locations. For one of the last great Depot parties Ed brought in some talent, Fred Gianelli of the Psychic Tv crew, to completely blow our minds. Before they clamped down on security it was a miniature techno utopia for us."

Ed's First Friday jams elevated Babylon, the only nightclub downtown in the mid-1990s, to mythic status. Mike Marion was a bartender there, "We never had any fights, no guns, people weren't getting stabbed, it was all about peace, and love, unity and respect. And yeah, we did drugs, we did a lot of drugs. It was not uncommon for us to be there until noon the next day still spinning records and partying. But Ed was a pioneer, not in facilitating drug use, but a pioneer in bringing music that most of the modern world didn't know about and sharing it with everyone. And it changed people's lives."

Jeremy Elliott fell into the scene in 1995. "So all of a sudden 16-year old Jeremy, who was hanging out with gutter punks and going to Ska shows, meets two people from the Dixie and Shaun O'Connor and starts raving his ass off. They referred to me as a rave baby, because we were under 18 we had to wait until 2:30 to get into Babylon. But they would go until 5:00 or 7:00am sometimes, unleashing all these kids with big pants and huge pupils on Elm Street as the straights were trying to go to work."

The pitfalls of promoting events predicated to a great extent on the use of illegal psychoactives were many but there was an added element of danger for Ed LeBrun, his proclivity for inviting straight, high school aged rough trade back to his home for a lesson in the three D's— Drinks, Drugs, Destined to lead to sex. Ed's friend Shaun O'Connor recalls a Spins employee warning, "'One day one of these guys is going

to kill you.' And Ed, shrugging it off as Ed normally did with things, 'Eh, yeah, that's not gonna happen.'"

When Pupils Grow Too Big

In late 1998 Shaun O'Connor was joining Ed for early dinners at a casual dining chain on Wendover, "He was just leaving Spins and I'd be getting off work so we would go to Fuddruckers. He liked the hamburgers, liked to build it himself." Another reason, Babylon bartender Mike Marion was manager of that location. Following one of those visits Mike joked with busboy and recent Ragsdale High grad Zachary Grimes about being one of "Ed's boys." Grimes assumed, wrongly, that he knew about an incident that occurred between himself and LeBrun two years earlier.

Grimes

Mike Marion recalls that exchange, "Yes. It happened. I said it. It was rumored that Ed had encounters with young men. So in that conversation where we were talking about Ed and his parties I told Zac that I had recently been in his home. Zac nodded his head and stated that he had been there before and 'hung out' with Ed in the past. I gave him that wink and a smile saying, 'Oooohhhh, you're one of Ed's boys.' I didn't dwell on it or even think about it after that. I didn't realize that it bothered him at all. He didn't let it show. He just smiled and said, 'Naw man, nothin' like that.' And that was the end of it.

"Zac was cool but there was something about him that struck me as wrong. I knew he was a criminal. I didn't judge him for it, I never hung out with him socially but we laughed a lot at work. I remember one evening specifically, a friend of his came into the restaurant while Zac was working, gave him a backpack and just turned around and left. I'm a responsible restaurant manager, 'Let's see what you've got there, we can't have anything illegal. I want to see what's inside.' It was a hammer, a crowbar, and a screwdriver, that's it. We got into this conversation... he liked to break into cars and steal stereos. It didn't matter what a fun guy he was to be around, he had a darker side.

"Zac would talk about Ed LeBrun sometimes, we'd get in conversations at Fuddruckers. Ed had a really nice house, he put a lot of effort into that house and did an excellent job. I talked about the nice things that were in there, or lack of nice things, he had it very simple. I wasn't conspiring or anything like that I was just talking about this cool house I had seen. Meanwhile, back in Zac's head, I guess he's thinking, 'Huh, this is something I can rob.' That was the farthest thing from my mind. Completely irresponsible on my behalf, to talk about things like that with Zac."

Mike Marion was unaware of the true catalyst behind Grimes' frame of mind. Six months shy of his 17th birthday he had been lured to LeBrun's home by a member of his church youth group with the promise of, "a party of sorts with a wealthy guy who provided all the drugs for his get-togethers." Arriving at the tidy Wafco Mills condo it became abundantly clear this was going to be a party of three. After dropping ecstasy for the first time, two hits, and inhaling whippets, the semi-conscious 11th grader was carried to a bedroom for what's best left to your imagination. Still somewhat woozy the next morning Zac confronted his friend on the ride back about what had happened but was cut short, "You knew what the deal was." No, he didn't.

Zachary attempted to bury what uncalled-for memories festered, suppress the shame, but a yearning for retribution was fermenting. Encountering Ed at his workplace on a regular basis was an involuntary revisitation of the helplessness and humiliation associated with that night. Was Ed mocking, regaling his table mates with "Hey, I had that kid over there," whispering to his boss about it? Zac was sure of it.

In May of 1999, spotting LeBrun topping burgers with a friend, Grimes ducked into the kitchen to connoiter with a new hire manning the fry station. He'd discussed assaulting and robbing LeBrun with co-workers before but this was Robert Reid he was opening up to—a randy, disarmingly handsome 18-year old live wire who's steely gaze barely masked a percolating rage, no doubt resulting from frightening sexual abuse he'd endured as a young child. For the next three months Grimes and Reid convened with Zac's roommate Jonathon Coffey, fired from Fuddruckers and now bussing tables at Don Pablo's, to map out how they would enrich themselves at the expense of the music promoter. A Babylon habitué with deep set dark eyes that reflected a Buster Keaton-like cluelessness 19-year old Coffey was well aware of Ed's predilections, he had friends who traded sex for pills. Shaun

Reid

O'Connor recalls the effect Jon had on both sexes at the club, "Oh yeah, he was the heartthrob."

The 3 Fuddruckerteers bonded over those late night BS sessions. Jon told them about a scrapbook Ed was rumored to have tucked away with naked pictures of all the boys he'd drugged and had sex with. Zac wanted to get his hands on that. Robert Reid revealed himself to be a Ninja warrior, the embodiment of Joe Musashi from the arcade game 'Shinobi.' A native of Chicago, he boasted about being in a gang and leaving more than ten corpses on the ground. He'd do it again, didn't bother him one bit, happily recounting how he clubbed his alcoholic father to death with an iron pipe when he was 11-years old because the old man reared back to punch him (untrue but a great backstory nonetheless).

Coffey

On the night of August 15, 1999, Zachary Grimes turned to Jon Coffey and asked, "Hey, you want to put this plan in motion?" Coffey did. At 11:30 he picked up Robert Reid who was even more enthusiastic. Back at the apartment they filled a bag with what they'd need—taser, hammers, screwdrivers, and a crowbar in case a safe needed opening. Grimes produced a syringe he'd filled with glass cleaner, "I drew the Windex up and had seen it in a movie, 'Terminator 2.' In the movie a woman escaped a mental institution and used this to kill someone by putting it in his neck." Before heading out everyone laughed at designated boy-bait Robert as he pranced and preened in his tight green shirt and baggy jeans meant to entice their intended. Coffey obtained the address they'd need from Directory Assistance; Ed LeBrun hadn't lived in his home long enough to be in the phone book. Taking two cars they parked close to the newly built brick manse on Mayflower Drive in Sunset Hills.

Robert Reid stepped up to the small enclosed porch and rang the doorbell. When he explained his car had broken down and asked to come in to use the phone Ed, speaking through the closed door, recommended a nearby curb market instead. Reid returned to his waiting accomplices. "The mother fucker would not let me in the house. He wouldn't trust me." Suggesting another try later they drove to a convenience store on Tate Street to purchase a pack of Newports and a Mountain Dew. Inside the mini-mart Zachary Grimes greeted an acquaintance, cryptically hinting weird things were going down, "If anybody asks, you're my alibi."

Pulling behind the building to smoke menthols and wash down some "Mark McGwire pills" Zac had in the vehicle Coffey asked, "What are we doing here?" Grimes indicated he was tired, wanted to go home. Reid feared his co-conspirators were getting squishy, "Are we going to do this or not?" Coffey told them "I'll have a go of it," agreeing to approach the door but only if the others were directly behind him. They outfitted themselves with rubber gloves and trash bags stolen from work, Reid also had a boot sheathed blade, a 6 foot long black shoestring... and a dagger.

They rolled alongside the curb quietly, lights off, parking just beyond the driveway. Grimes slipped a panty hose over his face, Reid didn't have a mask. Coffey couldn't wear a disguise, his face was his in. Answering the bell LeBrun likely peered from the narrow windows adjacent to the entrance to see a young man he knew from the club with a brooding boy band look and plump BJLs. With the chain latched he cracked open the door. Coffey threw his shoulder against it, tearing off the latch. Placing Lebrun in a headlock they struggled but the teenager was much stronger than his small framed opponent.

In the seconds it took for Grimes and Reid to storm through the entrance the homeowner had been rendered defenseless on the dining room floor. Recognizing Robert Reid from their earlier encounter Ed cried out, "Oh no." Zac Grimes punched him once as Reid placed knees against Ed's neck to tie his hands behind his back, instructing the others, "Sweep the house." In an phony English accent Robert passed the incursion off as a simple robbery, one that would be over in a few minutes. He led LeBrun upstairs while the others ransacked.

Grimes testified, "Me and Jonathon Coffey started going through the rooms not finding anything in two rooms then eventually went to the back room. It was like a disco with glow lamps, pictures, and it also had a egg seat and I wanted, a wax lamp, and Jonathon wanted the turntables. We carried that stuff downstairs and I went back upstairs to get a picture."

Inside a Chameleon Twist Nintendo 64 box Coffey discovered prescription pills, 8 baggies of crystal meth and 6 tabs of X. Zac Grimes uncovered a box of coins. When LeBrun told him they had sentimental value, that his grandfather had gifted them to him, the burglar put them back.

Directing LeBrun to the living room Coffey put the pill bottle to his face and asked, "Where is the rest of this?" Confiscating more pain killers from a kitchen cabinet Ed implored them to, "Get it over with and get out of my house, take what you need and get out."

While the other two stacked their haul by the front door Robert Reid guided LeBrun back upstairs to the bedroom where he terrorized his victim with a dual-edged dagger, offering him two possible scenarios—take a tranquilizer so he can't see them leave or be put to death. Yanking the wallet from Ed's back pocket Reid asked for a pin number and got it. In his preposterous 'Clockwork Orange' affectation Robert posed the Hobson's choice again. Sedative or die. LeBrun, who remained passive throughout the ordeal, understood his hopeless situation. "I really don't have a choice." He swallowed the pill. That's when Robert brought out the syringe.

After injecting Windex into an artery Ed was shot up with air, then rubbing alcohol from the bathroom. Reid told LeBrun he needed another dose then handed the instrument over to Coffey, instructing him to find something appropriate.

Focusing his attention on the cleaning supplies under the kitchen sink Jonathon found just the right chemical for the task at hand, concentrated Simple Green, a solvent promising to eliminate even the toughest stains. He filled the syringe with the Kryptonite colored fluid then bolted back upstairs where Reid plunged the needle deep into Ed LeBrun's neck. Grimes and Coffey looked at each other, both thinking the same thing... events they should have known could spiral out of control were now playing out in the worst possible way.

Grimes told prosecutors, "Me and Jonathon went downstairs and I carried that wax lamp upstairs and put it back on the speaker and plugged it in. Jonathon put the turntables back to where he got them from. We realized Ed LeBrun was probably gonna end up dead at that point." Making their way towards the bedroom, "Ed was on the floor groggy and you could tell some pretty ill shit had just happened to him. As we were walking down the hallway I could hear Robert saying his ninja saying, 'The paths are my shadows and no one will see my face.' He had told me previous murders that he had been implicated in, that was [what] his group would say to someone before they killed him."

They each took Reid aside, pleading with him not to go through with it, to no avail. Ed had seen his face, could identify tattoos. Grimes testified, "I walked downstairs, turned around, saw Jonathon at the top by Ed LeBrun's room. Jonathon turned his head to the left like he couldn't believe what he just saw, then walked downstairs." What he witnessed was Reid straddling the 39-year old, plunging the dagger a dozen times into his chest and neck. As they fled the scene Grimes straighten out a small welcome mat that was displaced during their forced entry.

With Zac behind the wheel Robert Reid was exhilarated at "what a rush" it was taking a man's life, bragging that his skillfully inserted initial wound was directed at an area of the body that excretes endorphins so Ed would be high, rendering each subsequent stabbing painless.

Turning on to Page Street, Grimes and Reid remembered the satchel they brought with them and LeBrun's First Union Bank card had been left behind. Reversing course they reentered the house before rendezvousing with Coffey back at their Stonesthrow Homes lair where they snorted some crystal meth, then set out to ditch the evidence. Keying in the number 0664 they extracted $200.00 from an ATM at Super K-Mart then hit two more machines for the daily limit of $500. Combined with the cash taken from Ed's home that came to a little less than $1,600.

With the other two tweaking in the living room Zac slid into bed with his girlfriend around 4:15am and told her what had happened. The alarm was set for 6:30, he was scheduled to open at Fuddruckers. Robert didn't need to punch in until 3:00 that afternoon, after he got off work he met up with Zac and they drained LeBrun's account of another $500.00 before burning the debit card and receipts.

Ever hear that old cliche, the guilty always return to the scene of the crime? That's exactly what Robert Reid and Zac Grimes did the night after the manslaughter, coasting past a phalanx of GPD investigators still on the scene of one of the most grizzly homicides in recent memory. Members of the rave community took to the internet to swap theories over who and why, clubgoers flooded the police department with leads. Neighbors were aghast over the apparent random nature of the ferocious attack.

How 'Ya Gonna Keep 'Em Down on the Farm...

Bulging with Benjamins the three perps got inked at Forever Yours, scored some crystal meth outside of Babylon, then further feathered their nest by burglarizing a gun collector. Now armed with a cache of weapons they boosted a Family Dollar store on September 26th, netting $1,200 in cash and merchandise. That supermarket sweep made them anxious for another big score... and they were considering putting someone else in the ground.

Their buddy Curtis McAlister knew all about the LeBrun butchery, pretty much everybody in their circle did. Reid revealed details to anyone who listened, followed by an admonishment: "If you tell anybody I'll kill you." Impressed with Robert's purloining prowess Curtis was contemplating a heist of his own, a grab and dash to line his pockets and humiliate his asshole supervisor at the same time. On leave for a cut finger he conspired with Jon, Robert, and Zac about how to extract the $50-80,000 in cash the Olive Garden raked in every week adding, "The manager's a pussy." If the back door wasn't open as it sometimes was, plans were made to go in heavy through the front.

Coffey, Grimes, and Reid were cruising up and down High Point Road October 13, 1999, eyes out for a business to bust-out, when they observed Olive Garden's back door ajar. Grimes idled beside the dumpsters. Bandanas up like a John Wayne movie the other two stumbled through the back door, making so much noise Coffey wanted to call it off but Reid urged him ahead.

With Reid behind him Coffey politely knocked on the office door, pushed it open and pointed a gun at manager Lewis McGraw, "Where's the money?" McGraw looked down at the pile of cash on his desk, what was left in the registers after the night deposit had been made. Reid slid his knife across the terrified manager's back, "Shut the fuck up or you will get hurt," while Coffey urged him over and over, "Leave the guy alone. We need to go. We need to go." They made off with $2,500, a good portion of which Reid tried to swindle his compatriots out of while counting the loot.

When he learned of the caper McAlister was furious at these smooth criminals for going forward without him. He was, after all, the mastermind that made it possible for them to once again be hundred-aires. From that point on Curtis supplanted Zachary when Jon and Robert pulled their B&Es. Coins rained down in a Jamestown laundromat like a loose Vegas slot; a nighttime burglary of the Barnes & Noble at Oak Hollow Mall netted crates of Pokeman cards and Michael Jordan commemoratives.

None of this larcenous activity escaped the notice of the numerous law enforcement precincts these degenerates were thumbing their noses at. While they may have been wanted for dozens of felonies and misdemeanors what Reid, Coffey, and Grimes weren't suspected of was the murder of Ed LeBrun. During their 2 month long crime spree Greensboro detectives were confident they had the killer locked safely behind bars. In fact, GPD bagged their prey within the first 48 hours, even rounding up an accomplice, and did it without a shred of physical evidence linking them to the crime.

On the flip side: Railroading doesn't end at the Depot.

Robert Reid's demeanor during his trial

Reckonings

"I was unable to sleep the night I received your letter. A lot escapes the mind after so much time, whether it be repressed or just forgotten. It reminded me what a piece of shit I was. Regardless of what I intended or did at the behest of others doesn't change the fact crimes were committed, a man died, and my person was involved." Zachary Grimes has a lot to be remorseful about and plenty of time to think on it, he's serving a 30-year sentence for his part in the torture and murder of Ed LeBrun, the east coast's leading rave promoter.

Ed's First Friday events were legendary at Babylon, the only nightclub in Downtown Greensboro in 1994, an after dark beacon amidst a desolate no-man's land summoning amped-up ravers attracted by the biggest names in EDM: Sasha, Icey, Doc Martin, Huda Huda, Christopher Lawrence, Sneak, Supa DJ Dmitry, Micro, Mr. Bubble, Bjørn Svin, and Donald Glaude. Upwards of a thousand blissed-out whirling dervishes flowing in and out of 221 S. Elm Street, glow sticks twirling in each hand, furiously sucking on pacifiers, Vicks inhalers tucked into their back pockets, music blasting 130 beats per minute, humidity approaching monsoon levels.

"What's in the middle of I-95? Greensboro. Not to mention 85 from Charlotte." DJ Mr. Bill spun Progressive House at Babylon, "We had the biggest scene on the east coast, we were bigger than DC, we were bigger than Atlanta. Between Baltimore and Orlando, Greensboro was the spot. We owned it. Club kids would put themselves up somewhere and stay for a month because their favorite DJ was going to be here on the 15th. They'd crash at somebody's apartment and hang out in town for weeks."

Ground zero for MDMA, at Babylon everyone was rolling like church buses on Sunday. Young people huddled up and cuddled up along the hallways and in the more mellow upstairs lounge. DJ Mr. Bill explained, "Everybody that was in the know knew not to buy drugs at the club. You bought them like 3 days before, you made an arrangement. By the night they were sold out. People would show up from outside of Greensboro, the suburbs, and they're expecting to find the drug of their choice and it's gone. You buy on a Tuesday if the party's on a Friday."

While claiming not to be a typical raver a male student who frequented

First Fridays revealed to the Duke Chronicle why he actually *was* the archetypal Babylonian, "The music is a mirror of your roll. Even if you aren't rolling, it's a mirror of what you feel like. When the music's pumping you feel like you're gonna fly. You stop, and breathe and then it builds. If it kept going without a pause, you wouldn't be able to handle it. I go and have guys massage me and girls kiss me at the same time. You completely leave the rest of the world. On the dance floor you focus on people's eyes. I feel like I can see through them. I don't know what people's lives are like outside of the rave. But inside, everyone's always happy. The day after you're exhausted. You don't really eat anything. You just feel drained. It's depressing a few days after."

When officers frisked an X dealer and found bags of pills that didn't resemble any illegal substance they'd ever seen before they had no reason to believe it wasn't Vitamin C that enabled kids to dance longer. It was a good 4 years after Babylon opened before police learned to ID ecstasy. One scenester described the action outside the club, "I was in a car with a guy who had an ounce of cocaine bumping everybody in the parking lot, he had a cooler full of liquid LSD, selling it for $80.00 a bottle. We had a good time for a long time getting away with doing a lot of things we should never have been getting away with doing, and we did it right under the nose of the police department."

DJ Mr. Bill remembers, "There was a guy working security, an off-duty police officer. Friday nights, Saturday nights, he'd go out in the parking lot and confiscate all the liquor he could find and take it home, that was his bonus.

"I was out of town but my girlfriend told me about this the next day—the staff and the owners one night decided to have fun and locked the front doors. They took turns DJing, the staff was on the floor, some got naked some didn't. It was like a party of five, more or less. My girlfriend was dancing butt naked on the little platform under the disco ball. She was like, 'I've got the whole place to myself!' I'm kicking myself 'cause I missed it. I asked her, 'What's that all about?' 'Oh, they do that all the time.'"

Besides promoting First Friday parties Ed LeBrun owned Spins Records & Tapes, the Triad's dance music roundhouse. William Shea was a manager there, he posted this on a message board: "No, Ed did not start the scene in NC. What he did do was take it to the next level. When I learned of the music in 1992, the Trim Shop was in full swing. Folks from all over the east coast, New York, Florida, Washington, Georgia, you name it. Literally thousands of people at those events, some driving hundreds of miles to pack into a dirty ass warehouse to see a few local DJ's. It was absolute madness, the coolest thing I had ever experienced.

"From there to Babylon and First Friday, one of the longest running monthlies on the east coast. Longer than Buzz, Fever, NASA. DJ's would cancel gigs to come to Babylon because they loved playing there. They could count on good sound, good lights, a good crowd. [LeBrun] was always up front with the talent, Paul Van Dyk came to First Friday in 1995. Ed was one of the first in the USA to book Misstress Barbara and the first to book 1.8.7. after Joe became Jordana. The DJ's loved it here."

At 2:30am doors would open for underage ravers, parents would drop their teens off at the club, presumably unaware of the goings on inside. Ed's friend Shaun O'Connor pinpoints when things turned sour, "This younger crowd came in like '97, '98. You had a bad bunch of people going around that would come in from out of town, make themselves look real cool, and sell a bunch of fake drugs. They'd be there for like an hour, sell all their drugs and leave, you'd never see them again. Greensboro tightened up after that and became more cliquish, people started hanging out at the sofa bar."

When LeBrun didn't show up for work on August 16, 1999 his employees knew right away something was amiss. Chris Kennedy explains, "No matter what happened over the weekend Ed religiously came in to Spins on Mondays to do all his orders for records, mainly the vinyl for the DJ's. When he didn't show up to do it, that is what prompted William Shea to go by his house to check on him."

Andy Guthrie wrote online, "I, along with my boyfriend, found Ed the day he died. I found him face down on the floor in his bedroom, blood soaked into the carpet all around him. I can still vividly recall staring at his brilliant white socks while I straddled his dead body to call the police."

DJ Mr. Bill will never forget that afternoon, "I was working at Elizabeth's and everyone said, 'Turn on the news.' We had TVs in the restaurant so I could see that it was for real. I'm like, 'You gotta be kidding me, I saw him last night.' Elizabeth's was in the same shopping center, we were like 6 doors down from Spins. I waited until my lunch break, I walked up to Spins, the doors were locked but there were already flowers and cards, a memorial. So I did the same thing, I left flowers and cards. They were shut at least 3 days, maybe the entire week. It was tough."

To Project and Serve:
They Don't Call this Guilty County for Nothing

Sunset Hills was on edge, understandably so, when news spread of the heinous attack just a block from the UNCG campus. Families slept easier when, two days later, a suspect was hauled in for questioning based on a tip and a blurry surveillance photo that matched the culprit, at least to the satisfaction of lead detective David Spagnola who wrenched a confession from 19-year old twink Tim Laney, not for murder but for using the decedent's ATM card. That admission of guilt put Laney at the center of the crime. Now the detective needed a name, who gave him the card? Laney implicated his friend Josh Gordon who was quickly jailed.

It was front page news when the arrests were made, sweet music to Zachary Grimes, Jonathon Coffey, and the guy who actually stabbed LeBrun to death, Robert Reid. They were in the clear. Perhaps Reid was the shadowy Shinobi Warrior he claimed to be.

"Had Reid said, 'Let's go kill this man' neither Jon Coffey or I would have gone." Zachary Grimes detailed how his life descended into madness in the weeks following the morning of August 16, 1999. "After the murder of Ed LeBrun we were to meet the real Robert Reid. He had the charisma of a gifted politician. Reid became ever demanding, he wanted us to do more crimes with him. He knew that we knew he was capable of murder. Jon and I complied several times but we were in too deep. We started resisting doing things, our choices were limited and my girlfriend was scared to death.

"I was sidelined while Jon and Robert continued on [committing crimes]. Reid's threats and spell were wearing off. I was tired, I'd already been thrust further than I ever intended to go with the murder of Mr. LeBrun so I just stopped.

"I was trying to salvage what I believed was the left of my life. I was trying to put the pieces back together but every one I picked up would crumble into more. A line had been crossed that could not be uncrossed. As for Jon, he was deeply affected by being involved in a murder. I believe he knew time was running out and he just gave in to the downward spiral. Jon really was a good person, the extent of his crimes before meeting Robert Reid were taking drugs and maybe selling from time to time.

"Robert began to feel the tension and rising reluctance to his every little whim or crime he wanted to commit. Robert would come over when Kara O'Connor, Jon Coffey, Kenneth Kitts, and I were at the house. He went off about us not being loyal to him and not wanting to really 'build something.' He pulled a gun and started making threats about if we were to tell he would kill us or go to our family's homes and kill them. We knew he had no problem killing so the days leading up to the arrest were stressful. Robert shot a hole in the wall, narrowly missing Jon.

"Jon and Robert's spree would come to an end the night he stole my car, and in the days after [when he] would break into our apartment with two 16-year olds... his new crew and next to be enthralled in his charismatic clutches."

Robert Reid had a habit of boasting about his escapades to any random person then threatening their lives if they ever ratted him out. Busted with his mini-mob in the midst of a burglary in Jamestown he folded like a card table. Omitting any word of his central role in the whole affair he gave up Jon Coffey and Zac Grimes as LeBrun's assailants. The two were swept up and charged with first degree murder.

"I'm not sure who interrogated me. It was late at night when I was brought in and I had smoked weed and dosed a couple of hits." Things looked grim for Grimes, Reid fingered him as the sadist who stabbed the record store owner 12 times in the neck and chest, a premeditated rage and revenge attack. "The District Attorney's office truly believed I was the man who had killed Edward LeBrun. I would go before a Rule 24 hearing for the death penalty. I just knew Robert had won, his web of lies with a twist of truth was going to lead to my death."

To their credit detectives noticed almost immediately the version of events they were being fed wasn't adding up. Before he could be cut loose Robert Reid was charged with being an accessory to murder. It was only the ringleader's insatiable need to grandstand that allowed the truth to finally come out. Reid bragged to his roomie about his treacherous run of burglary, butchery, and bloodshed. How he was left-handed but had the ability to stab his victims to make it look like a rightie did it. His cell soldier ratted him out... don't they always? Tossing Reid's belongings the screws found a memoir containing key details about the homicide. Combined with letters sent to one of his high school English teachers detectives now had a clearer view of what really transpired.

Tim Laney, the original suspect in the LeBrun murder who 'celebrated' his 20th birthday during the 2 1/2 months he languished in lockup awaiting a trial date for capital murder, was roused from his cell on Friday, October 30th and abruptly and without explanation spat out on to the sidewalk. Another innocent man Josh Gordon had been sprung six weeks earlier but only after his lawyer demanded a hearing to ascertain exactly what investigators had against his client. Turns out there wasn't a shred of physical or credible circumstantial evidence against either man. Both had alibis never fully vetted.

Laney

The story Laney told the press days after his release was harrowing. A coerced confession after a 10 hour long grilling during which the suspect reportedly asked for a lawyer but was told, "This isn't TV." He had an alibi but detectives threatened his witness with life in prison if he didn't change his story. Laney was lied to about his family identifying him in the ATM photo, threatened with the death penalty—all perfectly legal, of course. (Well, except for the part about being denied a lawyer.) Police Capt. Jim Scifres was quoted as saying, "I admit it is not the norm for us to charge people [with first-degree murder charges] and then release them but when we get additional evidence sometimes that occurs." By "additional" the Captain apparently meant actual evidence.

Gordon

District Attorney Jim Kimel found the incident disturbing enough to suggest police start recording interrogations adding, "If a person asks for an attorney, even if they already waived counsel, you ought to stop questioning the person."

Ed's Day in Court

Coffey and Grimes pled to second-degree murder, agreeing to testify against Reid. Shaun O'Connor sat beside Ed LeBrun's father Sid in the courthouse, "Every day of the trial I was there. Robert Reid just sat there spinning his pen with a smug look on his face. I remember vividly Benny from Spins and I having to contain ourselves because all we could think of was taking that pen and sticking it into his neck and chest."

Assistant District Attorney Richard Panosh prosecuted the case for the state, "Ed LeBrun had dreams. He took those dreams and turned them into goals. He worked hard and turned them into a business.

"The defendant had fantasies. His fantasy... to become a Ninja Warrior. The defendant dreamed he would form his own little army. One of the things he wanted to become was an assassin, and unfortunately Mr. LeBrun became the object of his fantasy." Panosh hammered the point home by pounding the jury box 12 times, once for each slice of the dagger, to highlight not just the brutality and length of the assault but the dozen opportunities Reid had to stop.

The trial lasted more than two weeks, the defense declined to call any witnesses or allow the accused to take the stand. When the verdict was read LeBrun's family and friends were jubilant; tough guy Robert Reid openly wept into his tie. Never again to breathe the air of a free man he barely escaped the electric chair.

Nine months after one of the most depraved murders Greensboro was ever witness to, and following a daisy chain of low level drug busts, local law enforcement and the ABC Board put boots on what had become known as "Babyland" in a pre-dawn raid following a First Friday event in May of 2000. Pills, tabs, baggies and origamis filled with white powder carpeted the floor after club goers dropped their drugs to avoid a possession charge. Cops broomed up more than enough evidence to shutter the nightclub for good.

Zachary Grimes is halfway through his 30 year sentence, Jon Coffey faces another 20 years on ice. Grimes' letters to me are circumspect, riddled with regret: "Every day of this sentence I've been drug free, as the drugs started to be leeched from my body over time my mind started to heal. The pollution that helped magnify my ignorance and studied stupidity was now gone.

Reid Today

"I will never lose sight of the pain I've caused the people who loved [Ed LeBrun]. They never got to say goodbye and their last memory of him is tainted. It's so clear now, I just can't believe I was so stupid. I believe Robert Reid is a truly evil person, sadly our names will be used together as long as the internet exists. I can only pray he lives forever in this place that crushes every last thing you love."

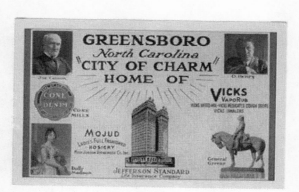

According to Greensboro's very first property census in 1829 the shopping district consisted of: "5 stores, 3 retail liquor stores, and a stud horse."

WEST MARKET STREET, GREENSBORO, N.C.

To Chief Wyrick
Love
Dear Friend
Jane Mansfield

My parents aboard
Bob Poole's party bus.

The

About the Author

Billy Ingram launched TVparty.com in 1997 and it quickly became one of the internet's hottest spots for entertainment and information, attracting millions of users a month. *TVparty!* was the first to broadcast clips of TV shows online.

In 2002 he released the best-selling book *TVparty: Television's Untold Tales* to rave reviews from around the world. He wrote and starred in a series for VH1, *Super Secret TV Formulas,* and two series on Bravo along with *The Christmas Special Christmas Special.*

Billy Ingram produced, art directed, conducted and transcribed dozens of interviews to craft the storyline for *Beyond Our Wildest Dreams*, an oral history of The Rat Pack Golddiggers in the 1970s. He also produced the Eisner Award nominated book *Dear John: The Alex Toth Book*. He authored a memoir in 2013, *Punk,* and the novel *Reverend Buck Goes to College* in 2014.

He was a designer on some of the most successful Academy Award campaigns, film trailers, and movie posters of all time, for stars like Harrison Ford, Barbra Streisand, Tom Cruise, Steven Spielberg and many others.

An internationally acclaimed actor, internet pioneer, artist, and writer, Billy Ingram stars in the indie motion picture *Lake of Fire* opening wide in 2015.

The author with his younger brother.

17467670R00084

Made in the USA
Middletown, DE
25 January 2015